# GOD SPOKE TO THEM

# God Spoke to Them

## Character studies of the Old Testament people

Peter Williams

GWASG BRYNTIRION PRESS

© Gwasg Bryntirion Press, 1998
First published 1998
ISBN 1 85049 139 9

Cover design by burgum boorman ltd

Published by Gwasg Bryntirion Press
Bryntirion, Bridgend CF31 4DX, Wales, UK
Printed by Interprint, Malta

# Contents

# Preface

My earlier book *Encounters with God* dealt with a number of New Testament characters. In the same vein the following biographical studies from the Old Testament are based on a series of sermons preached at Moordown Baptist Church, Bournemouth, during 1996. I have tried once again to present these 'lives' as faithfully as possible, including their triumphs and failings and drawing out the lessons and principles applicable to life in today's world.

What has amazed me as I have been writing this book is the wide variety of people God used and even blessed in pursuing his eternal purposes. Some were the kind of folk we would never have dreamed could have had a place in God's scheme of things. But that only serves to emphasise the fact of God's sovereignty in his dealings with mankind. Moreover, we must always keep in mind that some are included in the Bible to serve as a warning, whereas others are there for our encouragement. May God help us to strive after their virtues and not copy their faults and failings.

I owe a real debt of gratitude to Ruth and Brian Kerry for all the help they have given me in typing the manuscript and preparing it for publication.

Peter Williams
Bournemouth 1998

# 1
# Cain
## who murdered his brother

*Read Genesis 4:1-16; Hebrews 11:4; 1 John 3:12*

For most of us it is highly unlikely that we shall ever be remembered in history for anything we may have said or done that has had its impact upon the world. And whilst that cannot be said of Cain, we nevertheless do not envy him his place in history, since his name is proverbial as the man who committed the world's first murder. What was even worse, it was fratricide—the murder of his own brother. It is better, we feel, to live one's life unheralded and in total obscurity than to be remembered by future generations for an act as wicked as that. It is surely a sad commentary on the state of the human heart that whereas Cain was only the second man to live on the earth after Adam, sin had so dominated man's thinking and behaviour in that short time that it led Cain to murder his brother Abel.

> Now Cain said to his brother Abel, 'Let's go out to the field.' And while they were in the field, Cain attacked his brother Abel and killed him (Genesis 4:8).

## The character of true worship

It is a sad contradiction that this first murder in the history of the human race should have been associated with the worship of God.

9

Now Abel kept flocks, and Cain worked the soil. In the course of time Cain brought some of the fruits of the soil as an offering to the LORD. But Abel brought fat portions from some of the firstborn of his flock. The LORD looked with favour on Abel and his offering, but on Cain and his offering he did not look with favour. So Cain was very angry, and his face was downcast (Genesis 4:2-4).

The expression 'in the course of time' seems to indicate that the practice of bringing offerings to God in worship was already established, and so was something the brothers had done many times before. But this time it was different, since God accepted Abel's gift but rejected Cain's. The question is, Why? It is generally thought that Abel's offering was more acceptable because it was a lamb from the flock, and was therefore a blood sacrifice indicating the right approach to God. Cain, on the other hand, being an agriculturalist, could only bring the produce of the earth which God had previously cursed (Genesis 3:17), and therefore God rejected it.

I find that explanation totally unsatisfactory. After all, both occupations, shepherd and agriculturalist, were honourable in God's sight, and both the fruit of the earth and the lamb of the flock were products of God's creation. Moreover, in the developing worship of the Old Testament God encourages men to bring him the first-fruits of harvest as a measure of their gratitude for his providential care (Exodus 23:16). It seems that this is one of those instances where Scripture must be allowed to interpret Scripture. John says: 'Do not be like Cain, who belonged to the evil one and murdered his brother. And why did he murder him? Because his own actions were evil and his brother's were righteous' (1 John 3:12).

It is significant that John doesn't say that Cain was evil because he murdered his brother, but that he murdered his brother because he belonged to the evil one, the devil. In short, the disposition of Cain's heart was evil. He was not in a right spirit when he came before God in worship. There was already hatred in his heart towards Abel, perhaps because Abel was righteous in God's sight. Cain was jealous of Abel, and resented the close relationship he had with God which he himself lacked. Hebrews says: 'By faith Abel offered God a better sacrifice than Cain did. By faith he was commended as a righteous man, when God spoke well of his offerings' (Hebrews 11:4). Abel's offering and worship were based on faith in God. Cain, on the other hand, seems to have lacked such faith and was in a wrong spirit of worship when he came before God that day. That surely is why God rejected his offering.

## The giver, not the gift

All this teaches us an important lesson. It is not the gift but the giver that is important, not the worship itself but the spirit in which we bring our worship that pleases God and is acceptable in his sight. This is worth reflecting on, since today the form or pattern of our worship is one of the most contentious subjects among Christians. There are two things we can keep in mind that will help us with this.

(a) In the New Testament there is no specific pattern or blueprint for the right kind of worship service. The God who created us knows that we are all different in temperament and cultural background, and he therefore allows a large measure of flexibility.

(b) But God also makes it clear that worship must glorify him and must be directed to pleasing him rather than ourselves. When our Lord spoke to the woman of Samaria he had something very important to say about this.

'Sir,' the woman said, '. . . Our fathers worshipped on this mountain, but you Jews claim that the place where we must worship is in Jerusalem.' Jesus declared, 'Believe me, woman, a time is coming when you will worship the Father neither on this mountain nor in Jerusalem . . . God is spirit, and his worshippers must worship in spirit and in truth' (John 4:19-21,24).

The woman was concerned with the outward form of worship, 'this mountain' or 'Jerusalem', whereas the Lord Jesus emphasises the need of a right spirit before God. That was the point at which Cain failed.

## Growing resentment

The evil condition of Cain's heart and spirit is clearly seen in the bitter resentment towards Abel that continued to smoulder within him and was evident in his features.

Cain was very angry, and his face was downcast. Then the LORD said to Cain, 'Why are you angry? Why is your face downcast? If you do what is right, will you not be accepted? But if you do not do what is right, sin is crouching at your door; it desires to have you, but you must master it' (Genesis 4:5-7).

It seems that Cain had been brooding on the matter of his relationship with Abel and it was having a very negative effect on him. God was very gracious, however, and said to him, 'If you do what is right, will you not be accepted?' That can only mean that God was saying to him: 'If you deal with your spirit of bitterness and resentment towards Abel and make it up to him, then I will forgive you. But if you don't, then I must warn you, Cain, that that sinful spirit of yours is like a lurking beast within, waiting to spring and destroy you.' And that in fact is what happened. Cain did not deal with that resentful, jealous spirit within his heart, and the more he brooded on the matter, the stronger it became, until it sprang into a premeditated act of murder. 'Now Cain said to his brother Abel, "Let's go out to the field." And while they were in the field, Cain attacked his brother Abel and killed him' (Genesis 4:8).

Cain may have thought that out in the quietness of the field no one would witness his foul deed; but God witnessed it, just as he witnesses all our evil thoughts and deeds.

> Then the LORD said to Cain, 'Where is your brother Abel?' 'I don't know,' he replied. 'Am I my brother's keeper?' The LORD said, 'What have you done? Listen! your brother's blood cries out to me from the ground' (Genesis 4:9,10).

There are several important things here on which we need to fasten.

(a) First, it is foolish to think, as Cain did, that we can ever hide anything from God. One of God's greatest attributes is his omniscience. He knows everything. The Psalmist says: 'O LORD, you have searched me and you know me. You know when I sit and when I rise; you perceive my thoughts from afar' (Psalm 139:1,2). Even before he clothes his thoughts with words, God knows them. Depending on our relationship with God, this can be a frightening or a comforting thought. If we do not know God as our heavenly Father, it is frightening to think that every aspect of our lives, down to the tiniest detail, is open to his scrutiny. But when we live in loving relationship with God in Christ, then it is a comfort that he knows our longings and aspirations after holiness, our fears and loneliness, as well as the things that make us feel ashamed.

(b) Second, in the Bible, whenever God asks a question, as he did of Cain, it is never to seek information, since he knows everything. It has a pedagogic or teaching purpose. When God asked, 'Where is your brother Abel?', it was to bring home to Cain the wickedness of what he had done and to give him an opportunity to confess it. But in pride and ignorance he lied to God and said, 'I don't know. Am I my brother's keeper?' Therefore God had no alternative but to judge him.

(c) Third, Cain's attitude teaches us that when we become the victim of a jealous and resentful spirit, the thing to do is to deal with it immediately by repenting and asking God's forgiveness; otherwise we shall brood upon it until it festers and poisons the whole system, and it may lead us to do something we shall regret for the rest of our lives. The sin of resentment is like a lurking beast 'crouching' at the door of our heart and waiting to spring into action. Peter uses the same figure of sin as a lurking beast when he says: 'Your enemy the devil prowls around like a roaring lion looking for someone to devour' (1 Peter 5:8).

## God's judgment

God has assured Cain that he would be accepted if only he would deal with the spirit of evil in his heart (Genesis 4:7). But he rejected the offer of forgiveness and came under the judgment of God (Genesis 4:11-14). That tells us that we cannot sin with impunity. It also means that, as long as we reject the message of forgiveness and salvation in the gospel of Christ that alone makes us acceptable to God, we remain under his judgment.

But as long as we are in this life we are in the day of God's grace, and even to those who continue to reject the gospel,

God's mercy and forgiveness are still available. That indeed is the underlying meaning of the mark or 'sign' God put upon Cain. 'Then the LORD put a mark on Cain so that no-one who found him would kill him' (Genesis 4:15). People are sometimes perplexed by the idea that anyone could be around who might kill Cain, since he was only the second man on the earth after Adam. But Adam lived for 930 years and had other sons and daughters (Genesis 5:4,5). Cain himself also lived a long life, and during that time the earth's population was multiplying rapidly. God's mark on Cain, therefore, was a 'sign' both of his judgment and of his mercy in protecting Cain.

# 2
# Esau
## who lost so much and gained so little

*Read Genesis 25:19-34*

I think Esau must be the most stupid man in the Old Testament. He lost so much and gained so little in return. He threw away his precious birthright in return for a bowl of his favourite soup.

> Esau came in from the open country, famished. He said to Jacob, 'Quick, let me have some of that red stew!' . . . Jacob replied, 'First sell me your birthright.' 'Look, I am about to die,' Esau said. 'What good is the birthright to me?' . . . Then Jacob gave Esau some bread and some lentil stew. He ate and drank, and then got up and left. So Esau despised his birthright (Genesis 25:29-32,34).

What a stupid bargain to have made, you might think. And it certainly was. Yet it was the kind of action that was totally in keeping with Esau's character, which had been foretold by God even before his birth.

Esau was the elder of twin sons born to Isaac and Rebekah.

> Rebekah became pregnant. The babies jostled each other within her and she said, 'Why is this happening to me?' . . . The LORD said to her, 'Two nations are in your womb, and two peoples from within you will be separated; one people will be stronger than the other, and the older will serve the younger' (Genesis 25:21-23).

16

The struggle that began in the womb was to continue throughout the respective histories of the two nations that emerged from the two brothers, but it was from the line of Jacob that Christ the Messiah was to come.

## A sensual man

As the brothers grew to manhood the differences in character and temperament became increasingly evident. 'The boys grew up, and Esau became a skilful hunter, a man of the open country, while Jacob was a quiet man, staying among the tents' (Genesis 25:27). Esau was the rugged outdoor type much admired by some people. He would be today's macho man living life to the full, the man who would be found three of four evenings a week working out at the local sports centre and having a drink with his mates at the local pub. Esau was not a deliberately evil man, but he typifies the modern-day man of the world, sensual, earthbound and materialistic, intent on gratifying his appetites and desires, sexual and otherwise, and totally unspiritual and godless. His sensuality is evident, both in the way his physical appetite dominated him and from what the writer to the Hebrews says: 'See that no one is sexually immoral, or is godless like Esau, who for a single meal sold his inheritance rights as the oldest son' (Hebrews 12:16).

In today's society there are hundreds of thousands like Esau. They are often decent likeable people, but they are rooted in the things of earth, living only for the sensual and material experiences of life here and now, and without a single thought in their heads for God and the soul. In that sense, like Esau, they are despising their spiritual birthright as living souls made in the image of God and are selling it for the trivialities and 'fading dreams' of a passing world. Often such people are our neighbours, or we work with them, meet them socially or when shopping; we chat with them in the staff-room at school or on the ward in the hospital or on the college campus. Like Esau, they are not deliberately evil, but they all have this one thing in common—they are totally earthbound and the spiritual dimension of their souls means nothing to them.

From the gospel's standpoint they are, of course, to be pitied, because they are selling themselves short. As his creation God intended them for higher things. He meant them to have fellowship with himself and grow into the likeness of Christ, but instead of fulfilling their true potential both at the human and spiritual level, they remain stunted and impoverished, captivated by the earthy superficial glitter of our consumer society. Our Lord was so right when he said: 'What good will it be for a man if he gains the whole world, yet forfeits his soul?' (Matthew 16:26). And that is what these dear people are, lost souls. They have lost so much, and gained nothing but the judgment of God.

## Lack of discernment

Esau is also a warning to us about the lack of a spirit of discernment. For whatever reason, whether his own stupidity or animal appetite, he failed to discern between what was lasting and permanent, his birthright, and what was passing and ephemeral, the satisfaction of the moment. Just think what he did! '. . . for a single meal [he] sold his inheritance rights as the oldest son' (Hebrews 12:16). What a sense of values! But it was typical of the man, as we can see from the Genesis story.

> Once when Jacob was cooking some stew, Esau came in from the open country, famished. He said to Jacob, 'Quick, let me have some of that red stew! I'm famished' . . . Jacob replied,

'First sell me your birthright.' 'Look, I am about to die,' Esau said. 'What good is the birthright to me?' But Jacob said, 'Swear to me first.' So he swore an oath to him, selling his birthright to Jacob. Then Jacob gave Esau some bread and some lentil stew. He ate and drank, and then got up and left. So Esau despised his birthright (Genesis 25:29-34).

What a lack of discernment! His sensuality and appetite of the moment get the upper hand. He comes in from the fields, smells his favourite dish and with gross exaggeration says: 'Quick, let me have some of that red stew . . . I am about to die.' He must have it immediately, now! He can't wait, his passions and sensuality demand immediate satisfaction. In ten minutes or so he gulps down his bowl of lentil stew. 'He ate and drank, and then got up and left.' It was all over in minutes, the satisfaction of the passing moment in exchange for the permanent value of a lifetime—his birthright and all the blessing that would have come to him as the elder son.

What stupidity! Yet people are doing that all the time; they mortgage the joys of the future for the passing satisfaction of the present. A young person experiments with drugs, and an hour's delight and pleasure is followed by a lifetime of regret. A pastor, in the moments of indulgence, loses his sense of discernment and falls into sexual sin, with the result that twenty-five years of faithful ministry and people's trust are exchanged for a passing passion. But it is in relation to the soul's salvation that this lack of a spirit of discernment is especially tragic. People fail to discern between the temporary nature of this world and its pursuits, and the permanent joy and blessing of becoming a child of God and inheriting a home in heaven.

James puts it into perspective when he asks: 'What is your life? You are a mist that appears for a little while and then vanishes' (James 4:14). The brevity and frailty of life is something the Bible constantly keeps before us in order to help us exercise a right spirit of discernment between the passing and the permanent. 'Man born of woman is of few days and full of trouble. He springs up like a flower and withers away; like a fleeting shadow, he does not endure' (Job 14:1-2). Elsewhere life is said to be 'a tale that is told', 'a watch in the night', 'thread cut by the weaver's beam', 'a swift ship', 'a shepherd's tent removed'. All these metaphors describe life as something brief, fragile and ephemeral. There is an old saying, 'The world is a bridge; the wise man will pass over it, but he will not build his house on it.' Far too many people do just that. They build the house of their lives wholly on the things of this world, because they fail to discern between the passing and the permanent, between the things of time and the realities of eternity.

## The Christian's birthright

But it is not only the worldly person who sells himself short and, like Esau, despises his birthright by exchanging it for so little. The Christian too can lack the insight and discernment to make the most of his spiritual inheritance in Christ. John, in his first letter, describes our birthright in this way: 'Dear friends, now we are children of God, and what we will be has not yet been made known. But we know that when he appears, we shall be like him, for we shall see him as he is' (1 John 3:2). Peter elaborates further when he says:

> Praise be to the God and Father of our Lord Jesus Christ! In his great mercy he has given us new birth into a living hope through the resurrection of Jesus Christ from the dead, and into an inheritance that can never perish, spoil or fade—kept in heaven for you (1 Peter 1:3-4).

Our birthright in Christ is our salvation and the certainty of a home kept in heaven. What is more, if we really are God's children, born again of his Spirit, we can never lose that birthright of salvation. But, and this is where we need to be careful, we can lose much of the blessing that comes with it. We can lose the joy of our salvation and the purposefulness of our Christian life. We can lose our fellowship with God and our nearness to him as his children. We can lose our Christian friends and the encouragement and thrill of regular worship. We can lose our appreciation of God's Word and the comfort of prayer. All these too are a part of our spiritual birthright and inheritance, which rightly become ours when we are brought to new birth in Christ and enter into the family of God as his children.

But what can happen is that we exchange all this for what the world has to offer. We lose so much and gain so little. That is exactly what backsliding is: selling our birthright in Christ, allowing our spiritual life slowly to disintegrate as, little by little, we give way to the pull of the worldly spirit. Prayer drops away, regular worship drops away, Christian friends drop away as the secular encroaches more and more upon our life, until eventually, like the Prodigal Son in our Lord's parable, we end up in the far country far removed from our heavenly Father.

For what the Prodigal Son did was to squander his birthright. He came to his father one day and demanded his inheritance: 'The younger one said . . . "Father, give me my share of the estate." So he divided his property between them' (Luke 15:12). And what did he do with it? He sold it for the world's fast-living and glitzy lifestyle and ended up in a pigsty. True, he remained the son of his father through it all, for that was his birthright; but he lost all that went with it. And when he realised what a stupid thing he had done and what a bad bargain he had made, he said to himself in effect: 'What a fool I am! I've sold my inheritance and gained a pigsty. I'll go home and tell my father how sorry I am and how foolish I've been.' He did that, and his father forgave him and restored him to his rightful inheritance as his son.

What a wonderful forgiving Father we have! Even when we act as stupidly and shortsightedly as Esau did, despising our birthright and squandering our spiritual inheritance in Christ, he is always ready to forgive us when we repent and to restore us in the joy of our salvation. Let the backslider remember that.

> Who is a pardoning God like Thee?
> And who has grace so rich and free?

# 3
# Noah
### the boat builder

*Read Genesis 6–9 and Hebrews 11:7*

For many people the story of Noah and his ark is part of the world's mythology, or at best an ancient legend whose origins are lost in the mists of time but which is worth preserving as a colourful story to be told to our children. But this is not how the writers of the New Testament see it. For them it is sober history, and that explains why Noah is referred to among the other historical characters of Hebrews 11.

By faith Noah, when warned about things not yet seen, in holy fear built an ark to save his family. By his faith he condemned the world and became heir of the righteousness that comes by faith' (verse 7).

The apostle Peter also refers to Noah in both his letters.

. . . God waited patiently in the days of Noah while the ark was being built. In it only a few people, eight in all, were saved through water (1 Peter 3:20).

. . . [God] did not spare the ancient world when he brought the flood on its ungodly people, but protected Noah, a preacher of righteousness, and seven others (2 Peter 2:5).

But of greater importance is the fact that the Lord Jesus accepted the historical account of Noah and his ark and told us to learn from his faithfulness and heed his warning:

> As it was in the days of Noah, so it will be at the coming of the Son of Man. For in the days before the flood, people were eating and drinking, marrying and giving in marriage, up to the day Noah entered the ark; and they knew nothing about what would happen until the flood came and took them all away. That is how it will be at the coming of the Son of Man (Matthew 24:37-39).

## A man of mighty faith

Our verse in Hebrews says, 'By faith Noah . . . built an ark'. Our Lord speaks of 'great faith' (Luke 7:9) and 'little faith' (Matthews 8:26). Noah's was of the first kind. It had to be because of the age in which he was living. In Genesis 6 we get a vivid description of the godlessness of the times.

> The LORD saw how great man's wickedness on the earth had become, and that every inclination of the thoughts of his heart was only evil all the time (Genesis 6:5).

This seems to suggest that the corruption of society had become so grotesque and abnormal that God had no alternative but to bring upon it a cataclysmic judgment

> I will wipe mankind, whom I have created, from the face of the earth—men and animals, and creatures that move along the ground, and birds of the air—for I am grieved that I have made them (Genesis 6:7).

In a situation like that Noah had to have a faith in God that was mighty and equal to the uniqueness of the times. After all, no one had ever faced the fearful prospect of a worldwide flood before. It was an unprecedented situation and it called for an exceptional faith. And there is a sense in which the faith of every Christian has to be exceptional in the situation in which he finds himself. Sooner or later every believer has his 'evil day', that time or place or circumstance when he has to stand alone with God. He may recall others who have been in a similar situation and exercised a faith in God's power and goodness to see them through. But the circumstances are never exactly the same. The situation is peculiar to him and to his individual character and temperament, and he has to meet it with his own particular and exceptional brand of faith without any blueprint to follow, just as Noah had no pattern since there had never been a worldwide flood before.

This is especially true in the matter of salvation. No one can experience God's salvation in Christ through someone else's faith, such as believing parents or a godly home or belonging to a gospel-believing church. Your sinful condition is peculiar to you, and it must be your own particular and peculiar faith in Christ that must save you.

## A man with a warning

We are told in Hebrews that Noah received a word of warning from God to give to the people. 'By faith Noah, when warned about things not yet seen . . .' What were those things he was being warned about? They were the dreadful things associated with the cataclysmic flood that was to be God's judgment upon the wickedness of the age.

> So God said to Noah, 'I am going to put an end to all people, for the earth is filled with violence because of them. I am surely going to destroy both them and the earth' (Genesis 6:13).

Noah was a man with a message of warning and judgment for his day. Peter tells us that he was a 'preacher of righteousness' (2 Peter 2:5), and we can now see that a significant element in his preaching was a warning of God's judgment upon human depravity and wickedness.

It would seem from our Lord's words that such warning was needed, because the people of Noah's day were so absorbed with their materialism and pleasures that they were heedless and unconcerned about matters of the soul.

> For in the days before the flood, people were eating and drinking, marrying and giving in marriage, up to the day Noah entered the ark; and they knew nothing about what would happen until the flood came and took them all away (Matthew 24:38,39).

Noah looked beyond the surface appearances of the society of his day and could see a world rushing to its own doom and destruction, and he wanted to warn men and women.

The wheel has come full circle, and once again, as in Noah's day, the character of our society with its gross materialism, godlessness and inordinate absorption with pleasure and comfort foreshadows another cataclysmic judgment when Christ will come again to bring an end to this world's system and to usher in his eternal kingdom. That is the significance of our Lord's remark, 'As it was in the days of Noah, so it will be at the coming of the Son of Man.' Ours is a day when the Church and its preachers need to warn men and women of the imminent peril they are in. And yet what we find happening so often is a failure on the Church's part to make any mention of judgment or to declare the justice and severity of God towards humanity's sin and degradation. This is both to fail people and to deceive them by giving them a sense of false security, and all pastors and preachers who have failed to sound that warning will be accountable to God.

## A man who took God seriously

We are next told that Noah 'in holy fear built an ark to save his family'. That expression 'holy fear' is important. It means that Noah was moved with reverence and awe before the holy presence of God. In other words, he took God and his word seriously. When God told him to build an enormous craft, big enough to carry two of every kind of animal along with their foodstuff and provisions for himself and his family, he didn't treat it as a piece of fantasy. Perhaps many of us would have done just that. The whole thing seemed so absurd on the face of it—the very idea of a flood great enough to drown the whole world and its inhabitants! But it was no joke to Noah. He took God seriously and acted upon the word he received—'in holy fear [he] built an ark to save his family'.

The people of his own day certainly didn't take the matter seriously, as we have seen. They must have laughed at Noah and treated him as a weirdo when they saw him working on his clumsy craft, day after day, miles from the sea and without a cloud in the sky to suggest that a great flood was on the way. But Noah cared nothing for that. He had a holy fear of God and took to heart what God had said to him, and that was all that mattered. It reminds us of those words of the Lord Jesus: 'Do not be afraid of those who kill the body but cannot kill the soul. Rather, be afraid of the One who can destroy both soul and body in hell' (Matthew 10:28).

Do we take God seriously? Do we take the gospel seriously? Do we worship God with reverence and godly fear as we are told to do in the Scriptures? Noah didn't fear men because he feared God more. We can be very fearful of what people think about us and say about us. We can fear for our reputations and dread the thought of exposing ourselves to ridicule and contempt by making our Christian convictions known. In short, we take more seriously the thoughts and opinions of men than we do the thoughts of God.

There is a story about Latimer preaching before King Henry the Eighth and being aware that he was about to say something the king wouldn't like. So he soliloquised aloud, 'Latimer, Latime, be careful what you say: the king is here.' He then paused and continued, 'Latimer, Latimer, be careful what you say: the King of kings is here.' It was said at the burial of that mighty preacher of the gospel John Knox: 'Here lies one who feared God so much that he never feared the face of any man.'

## A man who preached salvation

What was it that kept Noah working on his ark year after year in spite of the mocking and jeers he must have encountered from the people of his time? It was the certain hope of salvation for himself and his family from the coming judgment of God in the flood. In holy fear he 'built an ark to save his family. By his faith he condemned the world and became heir of the righteousness that comes by faith.' We said earlier that as a preacher of righteousness Noah brought a message of warning and judgment in the face of the wickedness of his generation. But it was also a message of salvation, since he was warning men how to escape and be saved from the divine judgment coming upon the world. Every hammer-blow struck in building his craft was as clear and compelling as a voice urging the people to save themselves from the coming wrath.

We have already seen the need and necessity for the Church and its preachers to warn people of the impending judgment of God, as history runs down to its close in these last days and the coming of Christ draws nearer. To fail to do so is to deceive and delude people into a false sense of security. But the gospel is also a message of salvation, for we point out to people how they can escape the judgment of God upon sin and transgression. In answer to the question 'how shall we escape if we ignore such a great salvation?' (Hebrews 2:3) we must make it absolutely clear that there is no escape from eternal judgment apart from what God has done in providing a Saviour in the Lord Jesus Christ. Preaching of Christ in Acts Peter says: 'Salvation is found in no-one else, for there is no other name under heaven given to men by which we must be saved' (Acts 4:12).

It is said of Noah: 'By his faith he condemned the world and became heir of the righteousness that comes by faith.' What does that mean? Simply this. By taking God seriously and preaching faithfully the message of judgment and salvation, Noah was in fact condemning the people of his day by proving them wrong in disregarding his warning and rejecting the salvation God offered them. For what happened? They were all swept away by the flood and brought condemnation and destruction on their own souls. But Noah, through believing God, became heir of that eternal righteous inheritance in heaven which belongs to all who equally know and love God in the Lord Jesus Christ.

# 4
# Lot
## who began well but ended badly

*Read Genesis 12 & 13*

To my mind Lot is one of the saddest and most pitiable characters of the Old Testament. His story begins with such high hopes of the future, and yet it ends in disgrace and ignominy. In some ways he reminds us of Samson. He too began life on a high note of service for God, and yet it all ended on a note of failure. Yet both men loved God in their own way, whilst failing to realise their full potential as God's servants. That was especially true of Lot, who is described by the apostle Peter as a righteous man (2 Peter 2:7).

Speaking of God's judgment upon the city of Sodom, Peter says:

> . . . and if [God] rescued Lot, a righteous man, who was distressed by the filthy lives of lawless men (for that righteous man, living among them day after day, was tormented in his righteous soul by the lawless deeds he saw and heard) . . . (2 Peter 2:7-8).

So Lot was a righteous man, who truly belonged to God; but he mingled his godliness with a good deal of worldliness, as is evident from his living in the city of Sodom. In that sense we can speak of him as a representative man—he represents all those Christians who began well enough when they first committed their life in faith to Jesus Christ, but then the pull

of the world around them was too strong and gradually they
began to backslide into an unsatisfactory Christian life in
which they were trying to serve both God and Mammon. In
spite of the fact that our Lord teaches clearly that you cannot
do both at the same time, Christians nevertheless persist in
trying to do so. Lot's story is a warning about the consequences that can follow.

## Lot's bright beginning

The story begins in Genesis 12 when God called Abram to
leave his home in Chaldea or Babylonia and to set out on a
great pilgrimage of faith to the promised land of Canaan:

> The LORD had said to Abram, 'Leave your country, your
> people and your father's household and go to the land I
> will show you. I will make you into a great nation and I
> will bless you; I will make your name great, and you will
> be a blessing. I will bless those who bless you, and who-
> ever curses you I will curse; and all peoples on earth will
> be blessed through you.' So Abram left, as the LORD had
> told him; and Lot went with him (Genesis 12:1-4).

Lot, Abram's nephew (verse 5), must have been tremen-
dously excited as a young man setting out on a great adven-
ture of faith in the company of a godly man like his uncle
Abram. There is no reason whatever to suppose at this point
that he was not sincere in his faith and that God was not very
real to him. It is like that for any young person when beginning life as a newly committed Christian; it is a tremend-
ously exciting experience as a whole new life opens up
before one.

But on arrival at Canaan something happened which, I

believe, affected Lot for the worse and was the beginning of
his backsliding from God. It in no way excused his faithlessness, but it is a factor to be taken into account when studying
his life and character. What happened was this. On arrival in
Canaan there was an acute famine and Abram decided to
continue his journey down to Egypt where life would be easier. He ought not to have done that, since God had said he
would bring him to Canaan, not to Egypt, and as a result of
his disobedience he got into deep trouble and let God down.

> As he was about to enter Egypt, he said to his wife Sarai, 'I
> know what a beautiful woman you are. When the Egyp-
> tians see you, they will say, "This is his wife." Then they
> will kill me but will let you live. Say you are my sister, so
> that . . . my life will be spared because of you' (Genesis
> 12:11-13).

As the story unfolds, we see that Abram was saved only by
the intervention of God; but in the meantime his lying and
deception, and his readiness to let Sarai experience great distress and humiliation, had lost him his testimony before the
pagan Pharaoh as a God-fearing man (Genesis 12:14-20).

We can imagine what a profoundly disillusioning effect
this incident must have had upon the younger man. He
would have felt that he could no longer look up to his uncle
with the same respect for his godliness of character as he had
done previously. For when we move into the next chapter
(13) it is significant that tension had developed between them
and they were forced to separate. So what does all this teach
us?

Well, it is certainly reminding older Christians how careful they should be in the influence they exert upon those who
are younger in years and in their Christian faith. Within the
local church fellowship, young people should be able to look

up to older believers and respect them for their godliness of life and character and see them as role models for what a Christian ought to be. Abram failed in that. Likewise, when young people see mature Christians acting in a way that is not consistent with their profession of faith or their office in the church, then it can be very disillusioning for them and impede their spiritual progress and outlook. Needless to say, this does not excuse any moral or spiritual failure in the lives of young Christians, since in the end we are all personally responsible before God for the life we live. And that was true of Lot. We cannot excuse the drift in his life away from God from this point onwards in his story.

## When Mammon comes first

From the opening verses of chapter 13 it is evident that Abram had restored his relationship with God, for we are told in verse 4 that he returned to the altar he had previously built at Bethel and there he 'called on the name of the LORD'. But the experience in Egypt had left its mark on both men, because friction and tension now developed between them.

> Now Lot, who was moving about with Abram, also had flocks and herds . . . But the land could not support them while they stayed together, for their possessions were so great . . . And quarrelling arose between Abram's herdsmen and the herdsmen of Lot. The Canaanites . . . were also living in the land (Genesis 13:5-7).

We might have hoped that the increase in their material wealth would have caused both men to have praised and thanked God together. After all, Scripture teaches that 'Every good and perfect gift is from above, coming down from the Father' (James 1:17). As it was, their growing prosperity meant that the land was not big enough for both of them. And yet this was the very land to which God had brought them so that his people in the future could live there in peace and unity. It seems that Lot was chiefly to blame since Abram—as we shall see shortly—was very considerate to his nephew in resolving their differences.

But what a sad state of affairs it always is when material considerations come first in the life of the believer rather than the things of God. It is not that material things in themselves are bad or that God gets left out of the Christian's life altogether. No real Christian would ever do that. But the covetous spirit or the love of Mammon does mean that God has to compete with all the other things in our lives to get our full attention and to have his rightful place on the throne of our personality. That is why the Lord Jesus said, 'You cannot serve both God and Money' (Matthew 6:24).

Another sad feature of this tension between Abram and Lot was that it gave a bad witness to the surrounding pagan nations. 'The Canaanites and Perizzites were also living in the land at that time' (Genesis 13:7). The writer is saying by this note that through their bickering and quarrelling they were dishonouring the name of the true God they claimed to worship. And that again is a warning to believers that the pagan world is watching us. It watches our behaviour, our standards, our reaction to various situations, and it rightly expects us to be different from the accepted norms. After all, we claim to be different; we are God's people.

## Lot's choice

It was Abram who took the first step to resolve their differences, and it is evident at this point that a covetous, greedy spirit was already at work in Lot.

> So Abram said to Lot, 'Let's not have any quarrelling
> between you and me . . . for we are brothers. Is not the
> whole land before you? . . . If you go to the left, I'll go to
> the right; if you go to the right, I'll go to the left' (Genesis
> 13:8-9).

That was a gracious act on Abram's part and Lot needed no
urging to take him up on the offer.

> Lot looked up and saw that the whole plain of the Jordan
> was well watered, like the garden of the Lord . . . So Lot
> chose for himself the whole plain of the Jordan . . . and
> pitched his tents near Sodom (Genesis 13:10-12).

We can imagine the scheming brain of Lot working over-
time as he saw the lush, fertile pastures of the Jordan plain
that would fatten his sheep and cattle and make him richer
than he already was, and we can hear him saying to himself:
'I wasn't born yesterday. I know a good deal when I see one.
A man must take his chances in this life when they come.'
And without so much as a thought for the sadness of the situation, or the feelings of his uncle Abram and the fact of their
separation, he says: 'I'll take this, this is mine, all mine.' His
eye was on the main chance and on himself, not on God. And
the choice he made was to set the direction of the rest of his
life and take him still further from God.

There are certain choices we make in this life that can be
crucial for the direction we are to take in the future, especially
in relation to God in Christ and the way in which we serve
him. As believers we have to make our plans for the future
where our career or children are concerned. But the thing to
remember is that we do not make these important choices
with our eye solely on the main chance and material considerations. We should take God into our plans, tell him about

them and ask him to be gracious to us and close the door on any decisions we make which may seem to be to our benefit but are not in line with his will and purpose for us.

## Lot's deterioration

Following the choice he made we are told something very significant about Lot. 'Lot . . . pitched his tents near Sodom. Now the men of Sodom were wicked and were sinning greatly against the LORD' (Genesis 13:12,13). We know all about Sodom, how God later wiped it off the face of the earth as a judgment upon its wickedness and immorality (Genesis 19:23-25). Yet it was in the direction of these people that Lot chose not only to pitch his tents and set up home, but to set his sights for the future of himself and his family. Later in the story we read of Lot that 'he was living in Sodom' (Genesis 14:12). So a marked change had taken place over a period of time. Earlier he had lived 'near' Sodom, but now the pull and attraction of Sodom's life and society had drawn him to live in the city. Perhaps he thought that the city had benefits to offer his wife and daughters through its social life which would be distinctly preferable to the drab existence of life out on the plain. Whatever the reason, it was definitely a step downward and further away from God. But the drift didn't end there. In the story of God's judgment upon Sodom in chapter 19 we read that 'Lot was sitting in the gateway of the city'. That is a distinct phrase with technical overtones. The 'gateway' in the Old Testament was the place where the city elders or magistrates met to settle disputes and engage in judicial matters. But it was also the place where people met to enjoy gossip and social interaction.

It may have been that by this time Lot had been promoted to the position of city elder or magistrate, but we cannot be certain. But whatever his reason for sitting in the gateway of the city, it certainly shows that he was now fully accepted into its way of life. To all outward appearances he was right at home in one of the wickedest cities that ever disgraced the earth, and one upon which God brought a terrible judgment which destroyed it for ever. Indeed, it was only through the intercessory prayer of Abram (Genesis 18:22-23) and the intervention of God that Lot himself, along with his wife and family, was saved from the destruction. But he had paid a heavy price for his backsliding and moral deterioration. He lost everything in the process: his wife (Genesis 19:26), his wealth, his integrity, and above all the blessing of God which he had once known so fully. The last picture we have of Lot in the closing verses of chapter 19 is that of a man living in a mountain cave outside the city, isolated and lonely and in a drunken stupor, becoming the victim of an act of incest committed by his own daughters. What a pathetic end to a life that began with such promise!

The most unhappy person in the whole world must surely be the backslider, because once a man has tasted of the grace and goodness of God in his life he can never really be happy again in the ways of the secular world. The backslider lives in the grey territory of no man's land. He hovers between the claims of God upon him, since he can never shake off totally the influence of saving grace in the Lord Jesus, and the pagan values of the world by which he is trying to live at the same time. He doesn't belong fully to either, and therefore he can never know true peace and happiness. That was Lot's trouble. Speaking of Lot's life in Sodom, Peter says: '. . . for that righteous man, living among them day after day, was tormented in his righteous soul by the lawless deeds he saw and heard' (2 Peter 2:8).

The fact is that whilst, outwardly, Lot appeared to be

totally at home in Sodom and to be identified with its sinful lifestyle, there were times when he was deeply tormented in his soul because he knew in his heart that he was different from all that was going on around him. God still had a grip on his life. Years before, as a young man, he had known the high calling of God when he had set out with such high hopes in the company of his uncle Abram on the great pilgrimage of faith to the Promised Land. And as he remembered these things and reflected on them, he felt a sense of guilt and shame and suffered from profound unhappiness and restlessness. No, the backslider is not, and never can be, a truly happy and contented person. As long as he is unrepentant and far from God he will know a vague, undefined homesickness in his soul.

As to Lot's final salvation only God knows. But he reminds us of that man mentioned by Paul in 1 Corinthians 3:15—'he will suffer loss; he himself will be saved, but only as one escaping through the flames'.

# 5
# Moses
## who looked ahead

*Read Hebrews 11:23-28*

There is so much information on the life of Moses in the early parts of the Bible that a whole book could easily be written on his life alone. But in this chapter we intend confining ourselves to the overview given in these few verses in Hebrews 11. The facts surrounding Moses are well known. He was born to Hebrew parents in Egypt and as a baby was hidden by his mother in the bulrushes in an attempt to escape Pharaoh's command that every newly born Hebrew male child should be destroyed. Through the providence of God he was discovered and adopted by Pharaoh's daughter and brought up in the royal palace as an Egyptian prince. Later he was called of God to bring the Hebrews out of slavery and lead them to the Promised Land of Canaan. He was a mighty leader and at Mount Sinai was given by God the laws and commandments that shaped the Hebrew people into a nation. The Pentateuch or first five books of the Bible are attributed to his authorship and, like Abraham before him, he was known as the 'friend of God'. He died at the age of 120 and no one knew where he was buried.

## What he renounced

The first thing we learn from these verses is what Moses gave up in order to give himself more fully in the service of God.

'By faith Moses, when he had grown up, refused to be known as the son of Pharaoh's daughter' (Hebrews 11:24). In the Exodus story we are told that one day Moses 'went out to where his own people were and watched them at their hard labour' (Exodus 2:11). The phrase 'his own people' is a significant one, since it tells us that at the back of his mind Moses came to the realisation that he was not an Egyptian but one of God's people. How he came to this knowledge we don't know, but it may have been that his mother had kept in touch and told him of his godly heritage. But what is important is that after forty years of the luxurious lifestyle of a royal prince Moses turned his back upon it all and identified himself with the people of God. This was a tremendous amount to give up. After all, had he remained in Egypt he might have inherited the throne one day and become the next Pharaoh.

What does this say to us? Well, when we become Christian believers and God begins to move in our life by His Spirit, we must be prepared for a revolutionary change in our lifestyle and set ourselves to renounce the world, the flesh and the devil. In short, there will be certain things that will no longer have a place in our life, a certain kind of thinking we can no longer go along with and certain places and people we can no longer identify with, because they do not square with the new direction our life has taken. For Moses it meant he could no longer identify with being known as 'the son of Pharaoh's daughter' and all that meant by way of luxury and privilege as a royal prince.

Not all who profess to follow Christ are prepared for that. There is a worldly, cheap kind of Christian discipleship that makes no demands upon us and asks for no renunciation or sacrifice. It says in effect: 'Being a Christian need not change your life in any way. You can still do the things you used to do, think the way you used to think and go to the places you have always gone.' But that surely cannot be the new and radical life in Jesus Christ to which the gospel calls us when it says: 'if anyone is in Christ, he is a new creation; the old has gone, the new has come!' (2 Corinthians 5:17). And John says much the same thing: 'Do not love the world or anything in the world. If anyone loves the world, the love of the Father is not in him . . . The world and its desires pass away, but the man who does the will of God lives for ever' (1 John 2:15,17). John is clearly aware that there is a glitz and glamour to the world's way of life that can be very attractive to the believer and can seduce him from the love of God in Christ. But just as Moses turned his back on 'the treasures of Egypt' and identified himself wholly with the people of God, so the Christian must resist the tug of the world's way and its superficial lifestyle in order to give himself wholly to following Christ and serving his kingdom.

## The choice he made

As the awareness of God's presence became more acute in his life, Moses made a deliberate and calculated choice. 'He chose to be ill-treated along with the people of God rather than to enjoy the pleasures of sin for a short time. He regarded disgrace for the sake of Christ as of greater value than the treasures of Egypt . . .' (Hebrews 11:25-26). His decision to relinquish his royal status was not an emotional spasm. His refusal 'to be known as the son of Pharaoh's daughter' was now followed by a positive embracing of a totally different way of life. And that is characteristic of the Christian experience as well. The negative and positive must go together. We say no to the world in order to say yes to Christ. We 'refuse' the world's way so that we may 'accept' Christ's way with all that that entails.

For Moses it meant choosing obscurity in the desert instead of prominence in the palace; the life of a shepherd instead of the life of a prince; ill-treatment with the people of God instead of the pleasures of sin, and disgrace with the people of Christ rather than the treasures of Egypt. The words 'regarded disgrace for the sake of Christ' mean that he was willing to subject himself to the same scorn and reproach, the same ignominy and unpopularity that Christ himself was later subjected to during his earthly ministry. Moses endured the scorn and disgrace of his fellow Egyptians when he identified himself with God's people who were slaves.

There is such a thing as the reproach of the gospel. The writer to the Hebrews refers to this with an allusion to the sacrificial system of the Old Testament.

> The high priest carries the blood of animals into the Most Holy Place as a sin offering, but the bodies are burned outside the camp. And so Jesus also suffered outside the city gate . . . Let us, then, go to him outside the camp, bearing the disgrace he bore (Hebrews 13:11-13).

The carcass of the sacrificial animal was taken outside lest it pollute the camp, and Christ our sin-offering suffered 'outside the city gate' lest he pollute the dwelling of the people. That is the disgrace or reproach of the cross. He was despised and rejected by men.

And as followers of Christ we are to be willing, like Moses, to share in Christ's disgrace through whatever trouble or persecution our Christian witness may bring to us. Christ himself warned us this would happen. 'Blessed are you when people insult you, persecute you and falsely say all kinds of evil against you because of me' (Matthew 5:11). And Paul echoes that when he says, 'everyone who wants to live a godly life in Christ Jesus will be persecuted' (2 Timothy 3:12).

Such persecution need not be of the physical kind; there can be the chill of being ostracised in certain company because of our Christian convictions or the hurt inflicted through scorn and ridicule. Identification with God's cause and a strong vital witness will often bring hostility and resentment, because it reflects values and standards which make people feel uncomfortable or may even disturb their consciences. We can easily avoid the disgrace and reproach of the cross simply by being conformed to the world around us. But the choice has to be made one way or the other. We cannot have the saving friendship of the Lord Jesus Christ and the hearty endorsement of the world's friendship at the same time.

## The reward he received

We may wonder what it was that really moved Moses to renounce his royal upbringing and deliberately choose to suffer disgrace with the people of God. The answer is clear— '. . . because he was looking ahead to his reward. By faith he left Egypt, not fearing the king's anger; he persevered because he saw him who is invisible' (Hebrews 11:26,27). What was it that kept Moses going in the face of all the challenges and sufferings God had called him to? What was it that enabled him to persevere through all the trials of the wilderness march, when the people grumbled and complained under his leadership so that at times he was near the point of total exhaustion and defeat? It was one thing only: 'he was looking ahead to his reward'. He kept his eye, the eye of faith, on God himself and the promised rest of heaven: '. . . he persevered because he saw him who is invisible'. That sounds like a contradiction. How can we see God who is invisible? The answer must be, with the eye of faith.

In the Christian life there is a sense in which we are all

meant to be looking ahead to our eternal reward. That is to say, everything that happens to us, our daily experiences, our hopes and aspirations, our trials and sufferings, our joys and victories should all be seen against the backcloth of eternity. Moses had an eternal perspective on his daily life, and that is what kept him going. Of course there are those who dislike any talk about reward in connection with the Christian life. They try to be more spiritually minded than the Lord Jesus himself and they say in effect, 'Why talk about future reward? Isn't the living of the Christian life a sufficient reward in itself? Virtue and goodness is its own reward.' But that is not what the Bible teaches.

The Scriptures are quite emphatic that the certainty of eternal reward in heaven is the driving force that keeps us persevering in the Christian life. The Lord Jesus said: 'Rejoice and be glad, because great is your reward in heaven' (Matthew 5:12) and 'Be careful not to do your "acts of righteousness" before men, . . . If you do, you will have no reward from your Father in heaven' (Matthew 6:1). These and many other passages set out the principle that what should govern and direct our Christian life below is not simply the thought of the material rewards in return for daily work and effort, but the knowledge of the eternal reward that awaits us in heaven when this life is done. As the apostle says: 'we fix our eyes not on what is seen, but on what is unseen. For what is seen is temporary, but what is unseen is eternal' (2 Corinthians 4:18).

So we come ultimately to the question: Is it worth turning our back on all the treasures of this world's Egypt for the suffering and disgrace of the cross of Christ? And the answer must be, Of course it is. We are looking forward to our heavenly reward, and there is nothing this world holds that can compare with that.

There is a land of pure delight,
  Where saints immortal reign;
Infinite day excludes the night,
  And pleasures banish pain.
                Isaac Watts, 1674–1748

# 6
# Aaron
## the first high priest

*Read Exodus 4:10-17 and 32:1–26*

The main facts concerning the life and character of Aaron are scattered throughout the book of Exodus. He is also mentioned in Hebrews 5:4, where his calling as God's high priest is mentioned in relation to the Priesthood of Christ. We never seem to hear much about him, mainly because he is overshadowed by the immensely powerful figure of his younger brother Moses. Nevertheless, Aaron was an important figure in his own right and played a key role in the plan and purpose of God for his people.

## God's spokesman

Aaron's story begins in Exodus 4, where he is associated with his brother Moses in God's directive to bring his people out of slavery in Egypt. Moses felt he was not adequate for the task and had already given God several reasons why he would do better to choose someone else. But God was not to be put off, not even when Moses came up with his last objection: 'O Lord, I have never been eloquent . . . I am slow of speech and tongue' (Exodus 4:10). We cannot be sure, but Moses may have had some kind of speech impediment which would have been a great handicap in a leader. But God had an answer to that too, and by this time he was losing patience with Moses and his objections. This comes out clearly in what happened next:

> The LORD's anger burned against Moses and he said, 'What about your brother, Aaron the Levite? I know he can speak well. He is already on his way to meet you . . . I will help both of you speak and will teach you what to do. He will speak to the people for you, and it will be as if he were your mouth and as if you were God to him' (Exodus 4:14-16).

So the first thing to learn about Aaron is that he was chosen to be the voice of God, communicating the message of his truth and righteousness both to the Hebrew people and in the contest that would later take place with the Egyptian Pharaoh. Aaron was naturally gifted for this role since, unlike his younger brother, he was an eloquent speaker. There are many in our churches today who are naturally gifted in the art of speaking and are good communicators of God's Word. And I suppose there are also many among us who would like to be like that, having an easy flow of language and able to articulate clearly; but instead we may find it difficult to express ourselves clearly and quickly become tongue-tied. Others may find that it is not so much their words that are muddled but their thinking. If they get up to speak, either their mind goes blank or else their listeners are soon totally confused. It can all be very frustrating and disappointing, especially if one would like to follow Aaron and be God's spokesman to convey the message of the gospel to others.

But all that we have said about eloquence and fluency of speech applies only to the area of public speaking or preaching, and even then it is not always necessary in order to be a voice for God. When God called Jeremiah to be his spokesman his reply was: 'Ah, Sovereign LORD . . . I do not know how to speak; I am only a child' (Jeremiah 1:6). It seems he was not skilled in the art of public speaking, and yet he exercised a prophetic ministry for forty years in Judah. Even the great apostle Paul was not a particularly good speaker: 'For some say, "His letters are weighty and forceful, but in person he is unimpressive and his speaking amounts to nothing"' (2 Corinthians 10:10). When that mighty preacher John the Baptist was asked by the authorities who he was, he replied: 'I am the voice of one calling in the desert, "Make straight the way for the Lord"' (John 1:23). He was totally oblivious of himself, his preaching ability and eloqence, and was conscious only that he was a voice God could use for furthering his truth.

And that is all God asks of us in order to communicate the gospel to others, that we are willing to be a 'voice', an instrument he can use. Even in preaching it is never the eloquence of the preacher that saves people but the convicting work of the Holy Spirit. Indeed one could be the most eloquent preacher in the world and never be the means of bringing a single person into the kingdom of God. Looking back to the time he first visited them, Paul tells the Corinthian church that he was glad he didn't have the gift of eloquence, since it might have hindered the gospel. 'When I came to you, brothers, I did not come with eloquence or superior wisdom . . . For I resolved to know nothing . . . except Jesus Christ and him crucified' (1 Corinthians 2:1,2). Let us then forget the eloquence if the gift is not ours, and let us resolve to be simply a 'voice' that speaks a word for Jesus.

## The high priest

What sets Aaron apart as a distinctive character in the Old Testament was his calling to be God's high priest and to take the lead in the worship and sacrifical system of the sanctuary. God told Moses: 'Have Aaron your brother brought to you . . . with his sons . . . so that they may serve me as priests. Make sacred garments for your brother Aaron, to give him dignity and honour' (Exodus 28:1,2). The garments are described as 'sacred' or 'holy' because they symbolised both the holiness of God and the office of high priest as the mediator between God and the people in the offering of the blood sacrifices in the tabernacle. In this sense the writer to the Hebrews sees Aaron as a type or figure of the Lord Jesus Christ as our High Priest and Mediator through whom we approach God:

> No-one takes this honour upon himself; he must be called by God, just as Aaron was. So Christ also did not take upon himself the glory of becoming a high priest. But God said to him, 'You are my Son; today I have become your Father' (Hebrews 5:4,5).

But Aaron's high priesthood not only identifies him with the Lord Jesus Christ but also with us. In the New Testament believers are spoken of as a 'holy' and a 'royal' priesthood: 'you also . . . are being built into a spiritual house to be a holy priesthood, offering spiritual sacrifices acceptable to God through Jesus Christ' (1 Peter 2:5). And again: 'But you are . . . a royal priesthood . . . a people belonging to God, that you may declare the praises of him who called you out of darkness into his wonderful light' (1 Peter 2:9). All Christians are priests in the sense that we have free access to God through Christ without the need of any human mediation. We can 'approach the throne of grace with confidence, so that we may receive mercy and find grace to help us in our time of need' (Hebrews 4:16). We are a 'holy' priesthood because

God has called us in Christ and separated us to holiness of life. We are a 'royal' priesthood because we are the children of the heavenly King. As John says in Revelation, 'You have made them to be a kingdom of priests to serve our God, and they will reign on the earth' (Revelation 5:10).

Like Aaron who was greatly honoured and privileged to be chosen as God's high priest, so we too are greatly privileged and honoured through our priesthood in Christ. But as with every privilege there is an accompanying responsibility.

Aaron had specific functions to carry out in relation to the worship of the sanctuary and the offering of the daily sacrifice. In the same way, according to Peter, the believer too has certain duties and functions attaching to his or her priestly calling. He mentions two. First, to offer 'spiritual sacrifices acceptable to God through Jesus Christ' (1 Peter 2:5). Ours are not 'animal' sacrifices like those of Aaron, but they are 'spiritual' and will include our lives, our work, our worship, prayers and praise. Looked at in this way, the worship services on a Sunday and weekday meetings for prayer and Bible study will not be an irksome duty but a joy and privilege. Second, we are to 'declare the praises of him who called you out of darkness into his wonderful light' (1 Peter 2:9). We are to mediate the gospel of Christ to the world through our preaching, evangelisation and personal witness.

## Aaron's weakness

In our study of Aaron this far we have seen the positive aspect of his character; but now we come to an incident in chapter 32 known as the episode of the golden calf which shows him in a very unfavourable light. Whatever people may think of the Bible, they can never say that it is not an honest book. It never whitewashes its characters but portrays their flaws and weaknesses as clearly as their virtues. This is quite intentional on God's part, since the people of the Bible are meant to serve as warnings to us as well as an inspiration.

When Moses was on Mount Sinai receiving the Law and Commandments from God, this is what happened down below:

> When the people saw that Moses was so long in coming down . . . they gathered round Aaron and said, 'Come, make us gods who will go before us' . . . Aaron answered . . . 'Take off the gold ear-rings that your wives, your sons and your daughters are wearing . . .' He took what they handed him and made it into an idol cast in the shape of a calf . . . Then they said, 'These are your gods, O Israel, who brought you up out of Egypt' (Exodus 32:1-4).

This lapse into pagan idolatry was directly attributable to Aaron and to his failure in leadership. What is especially significant is that, within a mere forty days while Moses was on the mountain, the people's desires had shifted from God to a pagan idol, and that in spite of the fact that they had witnessed God's mighty power in the miracles performed in Egypt and the parting of the Red Sea. Contrary to what is being taught in some evangelical circles today, signs and wonders are not the answer to weak faith—only a deeper understanding of God's truth is the answer to that.

But the most striking thing is the weakness of Aaron as high priest and leader. He allowed himself to become the victim of crowd pressure, and that is nearly always fatal in a leader. He was like putty in the hands of the people: 'they gathered round Aaron and said, "Come, make us gods who will go before us."' In almost every local church fellowship there will be an element, be it large or small, who will attempt to pressurise the pastor into doing certain things or directing his ministry in a certain way. But the Christian leader must never allow crowd pressure to become the determining factor in his ministry. Sometimes the pressure comes from the world or from our peers, and this is where the ordinary Christian believer needs to be strong. Paul puts it like this: 'Do not conform any longer to the pattern of this world, but be transformed by the renewing of your mind' (Romans 12:2). J. B. Phillips translates it: 'Do not let the world around you squeeze you into its own mould.' The believer must be strong in Christ in order to resist worldly pressures.

Aaron's weakness is also seen in his attempt at compromise.

> When Aaron saw this, he built an altar in front of the calf and announced, 'Tomorrow there will be a festival to the LORD.' So the next day the people rose early and sacrificed burnt offerings . . . Afterwards they sat down to eat and drink and got up to indulge in revelry (Exodus 32:5,6).

That was a blatant attempt on Aaron's part to please the people and at the same time to salve his own conscience by mixing elements of idol worship with the worship of the true God. He tried to spiritualise the proceedings by calling it a festival to the Lord. But it was a whitewash, and the idolatrous element quickly asserted itself as the events of the day degenerated into drunkenness and sexual licence. Paul refers to this incident and says we should learn from it that we cannot secularise and paganise the gospel in this way and expect God to find it acceptable.

> Do not be idolaters, as some of them were; as it is written: 'The people sat down to eat and drink and got up to indulge in pagan revelry.' We should not commit sexual immorality, as some of them did—and in one day twenty-three thousand of them died (1 Corinthians 10:7-8).

God has said clearly, 'I will not give my glory to another' (Isaiah 42:8).

When Moses came down from the mountain and confronted his brother, the weakness in Aaron's leadership is again very evident.

He said to Aaron, 'What did these people do to you, that you led them into such great sin?' 'Do not be angry, my lord,' Aaron answered. 'You know how prone these people are to evil. They said to me, "Make us gods who will go before us" . . . So I told them, "Whoever has any gold jewellery, take it off." Then they gave me the gold, and I threw it into the fire, and out came this calf!' (Exodus 32:21-24).

How pathetic! Did he actually think that Moses would believe him when he said: 'I threw it into the fire and out came this calf'? And isn't it despicable, the way in which he tried to put the blame on the people instead of admitting that he had failed to exert strong leadership and discipline? We seem to be suffering from a similar failure in leadership in our country today, in politics, in social and educational life and in the Church.

Church leaders and pastors are especially to be blamed in this respect, since so many of them have failed to give people the spiritual and moral guidelines they need. Satan is very active today attacking and plundering the Church and undermining her credibility in the world, and much of it is due to a failure in leadership. When our Lord gave his famous discourse on the Good Shepherd (John 10) he was addressing himself in the first instance to the church leaders of his own day, whom he describes in the previous chapter (John 9:39,40) as spiritually blind. They were the false shepherds, the thieves and robbers of chapter 10 who were robbing men's souls of the truth of God. So it is today; many church leaders are robbing people of the truth of the gospel and substituting their own man-made ideas in place of God's Word. The true shepherd of this chapter, on the other hand, feeds the flock of God and leads them out to pasture.

In spite of his high and holy calling as high priest, Aaron, as we have seen, was human and sinful and committed many transgressions. The same is true of all who serve in the leadership role in the Church, especially pastors. But Aaron recognised his failure and weakness and truly repented of it, and when he died at the great age of one hundred and twenty-three he was greatly mourned by the people.

# 7
# Miriam
### a jealous woman

*Read Numbers 12*

We are not told a great deal about Miriam in the Bible, but her story, which appears within the wider context of the life of Moses, is told in order to warn us against the evil of a spirit of jealousy. She was the daughter of Amram and Jochebed and the sister of Aaron and Moses (Numbers 26:59).

## Her initiative

Miriam is first brought to our attention in connection with the birth of her baby brother Moses recorded in Exodus 2. Pharaoh, in an attempt to limit the number of Hebrews in Egypt, had commanded that every male Hebrew child that was born should be thrown into the Nile. Jochebed (see Exodus 6:20; Numbers 26:59) was determined, so far as she was able, to preserve the life of her child Moses, and when she could hide him no longer she put him in a pitch-lined basket and placed it among the reeds along the bank of the Nile. Miriam was left to keep watch from a safe distance to see what would happen.

> Then Pharaoh's daughter went down to the Nile to bathe, and her attendants were walking along the river bank. She saw the basket among the reeds and sent her slave girl to

get it. She opened it and saw the baby. He was crying, and she felt sorry for him. 'This is one of the Hebrew babies', she said. Then his sister asked Pharaoh's daughter, 'Shall I go and get one of the Hebrew women to nurse the baby for you?' 'Yes, go,' she answered. And the girl went and got the baby's mother (Exodus 2:5-8).

Miriam was a bright and intelligent girl, and by exercising her initiative and sound common sense she not only saved the life of the infant Moses but made it possible for his own mother to have a direct influence upon him during his early years. Indeed I believe this may help to explain what we are told in Exodus 2:11. 'One day, after Moses had grown up, he went out to where his own people were and watched them at their hard labour.' How did he come to the realisation that he was a Hebrew, one of God's own people, and not an Egyptian? Was it that Jochebed his mother taught him the things of God when he was a little child in her care? But the point is that this, and everything else to do with Moses which so powerfully influenced the history of God's people, hinges on the initiative shown by Miriam at the time of his birth. This is something we can learn from her.

Among the many parables of the Lord Jesus there is one that often causes Christian people a lot of perplexity. It is the parable of the Shrewd Manager (Luke 16). Here is a manager in charge of a vast estate who gets into trouble when his master asks him to account for his dealings. The fact was that he had been siphoning off money into his own account for years. To get out of the mess he was in, he persuaded the workers on the estate to forge their bills, making it look as if they had bought less than they really had. The Lord ends the parable with these words: 'The master commended the dishonest manager because he had acted shrewdly.' He then draws the lesson: 'For the people of this world are more shrewd in dealing with their own kind than are the people of the light' (Luke 16:8).

Christians get perplexed because it seems that the Lord Jesus is commending the steward's dishonesty. But that is not so. It is not his dishonesty that the steward's master is commending, but his initiative and shrewdness in getting himself out of a tight spot—just as Miriam's initiative and ingenuity got her baby brother out of a tight spot. Furthermore, our Lord looks at the steward's keen-wittedness and enterprising nature and says that the people of the world are wiser in this respect than Christian believers. He meant that in the affairs of God's kingdom believers do not show the foresight and initiative that the worldly man shows in business and the affairs of this life.

God wants us as his people to be as keen and clever, as quick-witted and creative in winning souls and pushing forward the frontiers of his kingdom, as others are in the service of Mammon. For let's face it, there are so many churches that are static and moribund. They seem to show no initiative or enterprise in getting the gospel out to the wider world. They devise no strategy of evangelism for reaching people in the local community, and they are far too parochial in their thinking. God cannot be pleased with that. He wants us surely to be wide awake and inventive, and as mentally fertile as we can be in serving and glorifying him. In her consecration hymn Francis Ridley Havergal talks about giving our 'silver and gold' to God, but then she has the lines,

> Take my intellect and use
> Every power as Thou shalt choose.

Among those powers to be sanctified and consecrated in the cause of God are initiative, ingenuity and enterprise.

## Miriam the prophetess

We have a further glimpse of Miriam later in life, when she leads the women of Israel in the song celebrating God's victory over Pharaoh and his army at the Red Sea.

> Then Miriam the prophetess, Aaron's sister, took a tambourine in her hand, and all the women followed her, with tambourines and dancing. Miriam sang to them:
>
>> Sing to the LORD,
>>     for he is highly exalted.
>> The horse and its rider
>>     he has hurled into the sea.
>>           (Exodus 15:20,21)

Miriam was clearly regarded as their leader by the Israelite women, but what is particularly interesting is the description of her as a 'prophetess'. Whether this prophetic gift meant that it was she who composed the ode to victory given in Exodus 15 we cannot say. But it might well have been the case, since the theme and focus of the poem is to set forth the majesty of God in overthrowing the power and pride of Egypt. And that is a distinct part of the function of a prophet or prophetess—to be God's mouthpiece. In Numbers 12:2 Miriam affirms that the prophetic gift had been given both to herself and to her brother Aaron. 'Has the LORD spoken only through Moses?' they asked. 'Hasn't he also spoken through us?' He had indeed, for that is one of the characteristics of the prophet—to be a 'forthteller' of God's word as well as a 'foreteller' of events to come. In this respect she is one of just four women referred to in the Old Testament as a 'prophetess'. The others are Deborah, 'a mother in Israel' (Judges 5:7); Huldah who spoke God's word to king Josiah (2 Kings 22:14), and Noadiah who tried to intimidate Nehemiah (Nehemiah 6:14).

All this goes to show what an influential and gifted woman Miriam was, and how God must have used her powerfully, alongside her two eminent brothers, to minister forth His will and His word to the people of Israel, and especially among the women. How sad, therefore, that she was not content with the prominent role God had given her but allowed a spirit of jealousy to invade her heart, causing disruption in the camp and great hurt to her renowned brother Moses.

## The spirit of jealousy

On the face of it, Miriam's rebellion against Moses, along with that of her brother Aaron, seems to have been caused by his marriage to a foreign woman. 'Miriam and Aaron began to talk against Moses because of his Cushite wife, for he had married a Cushite' (Numbers 12:1). Although Aaron is associated with her in the opposition to Moses, it is clear that Miriam was the chief offender and the more dominant personality, since it is upon her that God's judgment falls (Numbers 12:10). The truth was that the objection to the marriage was only a cover and pretext for her greater offence, which was her spirit of jealousy in connection with God's choice of Moses as leader. 'Has the LORD spoken only through Moses?' they asked. 'Hasn't he also spoken through us?' And the LORD heard this' (Numbers 12:2).

That a jealous spirit in a person is something God hates is evident from the severity of the judgment he brought upon Miriam.

The anger of the LORD burned against them . . . When the cloud lifted from above the Tent, there stood Miriam—

leprous, like snow. Aaron turned towards her and saw that she had leprosy; and he said to Moses, 'Please, my lord, do not hold against us the sin we have so foolishly committed' (Numbers 12:9-11).

Jealousy is a sin, a green-eyed monster that can be destructive in its effects. It is almost impossible to live with it if you are its object.

It is not always bad, however. There is a jealousy that is healthy and proper and a real part of true love, as we shall see in a moment. But it becomes wrong and evil when it contains the elements of resentment towards others and envy of what they have and are. Worse still, it breeds discontent and unhappiness in the heart. That was Miriam's trouble; she could not accept the role of second place to Moses and was envious of the special authority God had given him. We get the impression that this spirit of jealousy and discontent had been nagging away at her for some considerable time, making her deeply unhappy and miserable, and she used the occasion of Moses' marriage as a pretext to express her true feelings.

The Psalmist knew something of this spirit of jealousy and envy that can invade the heart, causing deep unhappiness and discontent. In his case it was jealousy of the material well-being of others, especially the wicked. 'But as for me, my feet had almost slipped; I had nearly lost my foothold. For I envied the arrogant when I saw the prosperity of the wicked' (Psalm 73:2-3). He says in effect that he had become so obsessed by a spirit of envy and resentment that he almost lost his faith in God. And he goes on to warn us in the Psalm that when we see others, even godless people, enjoying so much of the good things of this life, we should not fret about it and make ourselves unhappy and discontented. Above all, we should never be tempted to want to be like them, or our spiritual life will become embittered, empty and useless.

There is, however, another aspect to all this. Like most other emotions, jealousy has a positive side to it and is widely attributed in the Bible to God himself. The second commandment reads:

> You shall not make for yourself an idol in the form of anything in heaven above or on the earth beneath or in the waters below. You shall not bow down to them or worship them; for I, the LORD your God, am a jealous God . . . (Exodus 20:4-5).

In that context jealousy is an expression of God's love for his people. He has a covenant relationship with them like the marriage relationship between a husband and wife, and he guards that relationship from intrusion by any other form of worship in the hearts of his people. If a husband or wife felt no sense of jealousy at the intrusion of a third party into the relationship, it would clearly indicate that they did not value their marriage in the way they should.

But it works both ways. If God is jealous on our behalf, are we jealous for him? In the Bible another word for jealous is 'zealous'. In the Authorised Version Elijah says to God, 'I have been very jealous for the LORD God of hosts . . .' (1 Kings 19:10). The New International Version translates, 'I have been very zealous for the LORD God Almighty.' Both are saying the same thing. Elijah had a jealous love for God at a time when his cause was dishonoured in the nation and his worship despised. He was zealous in defending God's cause. Are we jealous for the cause of the gospel? Are we zealous in promoting the truth of God's Word against the flood of evil that washes all around us today? A Christian may be excused many things, a lack of intellect or talent or a forceful personality, but no believer can be excused a lack of zeal in the work of God. God loves us with a jealous love, and he wants us to love him in the same way.

# 8
# Joshua
## God's soldier

*Read Numbers 27 and Joshua 1*

Joshua was first and foremost a soldier, a military strategist and leader who planned the battles that led to the conquest of Canaan. The book that bears his name is the story of how Joshua was commissioned by God to take Canaan from the pagan nations as part of the programme of God's redemption for his people at that particular period in history. Joshua therefore is more than a great soldier—he was God's chosen servant. He reminds us of another outstanding military figure nearer our own times who was also eminently a godly man, General Gordon of Khartoum. In his biography of Gordon, John Pollock quotes the tribute paid to him at the time of his death by his contemporary general, Lord Wolseley:

> . . . if God ever granted the gift of inspiration in our day to men, I know of no one more suited from the purity of his life, his intense faith in God and in Christ, and from what I may call his close communion at all hours of his daily life with his God, to have received such a commission from the Almighty.

## The making of a leader

Joshua's name originally was Hoshea, which means 'salvation'; but this was changed by Moses (Numbers 13:16) to

Joshua, meaning 'God is salvation'. This corresponds in the New Testament to the name 'Jesus' given by the angel to Joseph with the words, 'because he will save his people from their sins' (Matthew 1:21). In the light of this there are those who see in Joshua a type of the Lord Jesus Christ as our Saviour. Without pushing the type too far, there is a real sense in which Joshua was indeed the saviour of God's people in bringing them into their inheritance in the promised land of Canaan, just as Christ brings us through the gift of salvation into our inheritance in heaven (see 1 Peter 1:4).

Joshua was certainly a man of God's choice, for when we read in the opening verses of his book that 'the LORD said to Joshua . . . "Moses my servant is dead. Now then . . . get ready to cross the Jordan River into the land I am about to give . . . to the Israelites"', this was not a case of God thrusting him suddenly into a leadership role. There was a long history of preparation behind this call to become the successor of Moses and the leader of God's people. In Numbers 11:28 we read of 'Joshua son of Nun, who had been Moses' assistant since youth'. So, from the time that he was a young man, God had been shaping and moulding Joshua's life in preparation for the day when he would succeed Moses.

As a young man he would have experienced the plagues in Egypt, the sufferings of God's people in slavery, the exodus under Moses, the crossing of the Red Sea and the destruction of Pharaoh's army. And all these great acts of God must undoubtedly have made a tremendous impression upon his young heart and mind, so that from his earliest days he was open to God's influence upon his life. Later, as he grew in faith and experience, he was given his first military command by Moses in the battle against the Amalekites.

The Amalekites came and attacked the Israelites at Rephidim. Moses said to Joshua, 'Choose some of our men and go out to fight the Amalekites. Tomorrow I will stand on top of the hill with the staff of God in my hands' (Exodus 17:8,9).

Joshua knew that it would not be the fighting skill of the Israelites that would bring victory, since they had none at this point in their history, but that it would be the result of the prevailing prayer of Moses. Later still, as the assistant of Moses, he accompanied him to the top of Mount Sinai to receive the commandments (Exodus 24:12-13). In our study of the character of Caleb we shall see that Joshua was also one of the twelve spies sent out by Moses to reconnoitre the city of Jericho, and he supported Caleb in making a positive report in spite of the opposition of their fellow spies (see pp.71-7). Finally, as the Israelites were nearing the border of Canaan and Moses was coming to the end of his life, Joshua was officially appointed by God as his successor.

So the LORD said to Moses, 'Take Joshua son of Nun, a man in whom is the Spirit, and lay your hand on him. Make him stand before Eleazar the priest and the entire assembly and commission him in their presence. Give him some of your authority so that the whole Israelite community will obey him' (Numbers 27:18-20).

The preparation of some forty years was now complete and Joshua entered into his duties as supreme leader.

What emerges from all this is a lesson especially for young Christian people. Joshua from his youth was open to the influence of God's calling in his life, and it is for pastors especially to guide their young people in the church in a similar direction. Young people may feel that they have leadership

potential, but that remains to be seen as they are encouraged
to let God in Christ take full control over their lives. David,
when he was caring for his father's sheep, didn't know that
he would become Israel's greatest king. Saul of Tarsus, when
a student under Gamaliel, didn't know that one day he
would become God's apostle to the Gentiles. The young
William Booth, working among the musty clothes of the
pawnbroker's shop, didn't know then that one day he would
become the founder and leader of the world's greatest
Christian social force in the Salvation Army. And neither did
Joshua know, when a young man enduring slavery in Egypt,
that one day he would succeed Moses as the leader of God's
people.

The key, I believe, to any young Christian becoming a
leader for God is what we are told about Joshua at his com-
missioning. He is described as 'a man in whom is the Spirit'
(Numbers 27:18). That is, he was a man who from his youth
was open to the indwelling power of God's Spirit. And it is
open to any young Christian to emulate him in that, for no
one has a monopoly of the Holy Spirit and the ways in which
he empowers and equips people for Christian service.

## Courage and strength

Any work done for God in Christ, or any leadership role we
adopt in his service, will always bring its own testings.
Leadership, in however small a way, always makes one a
target and focus of criticism and hostility. That is true even in
our service for God within the church fellowship. When the
mantle of Moses fell on Joshua he needed no one to tell him
that he had a hard act to follow. Moses was unique, a one-off
we might say, and Joshua knew he was in the hot seat. His
first test as supreme leader was soon to come in the conquest

of Canaan. This was an enormous task, with many battles to be fought before the promised land could be possessed. As we read the opening chapter of the book of Joshua we can imagine what his feelings were as he stood on the east bank of the river Jordan waiting to cross over and begin the battle. His feelings would have been a mixture of apprehension, excitement, fear and uncertainty. This was a moment when he needed a special infusion of strength and courage, and God gave it to him.

> As I was with Moses, so I will be with you; I will never leave you nor forsake you. Be strong and courageous, because you will lead these people to inherit the land I swore to their forefathers to give them (Joshua 1:5-6).

Notice, God's command was intended to spur Joshua into energy and to put new heart into him, but the onus is on Joshua himself. We shall see that the same was true of Gideon when we come to study his life. He is aware that the battle he is to fight against the pagan forces in Canaan is the Lord's battle, but he also knows that he is the one who has to fight it, and God will not do it for him. Joshua has to make his own battle plans and work out his own military strategy, such as sending out the spies to reconnoitre the land. And that principle applies to us as we engage in the warfare of the Spirit against the forces of paganism in today's world. Paul exhorts us to 'put on the full armour of God, so that when the day of evil comes, you may be able to stand your ground' (Ephesians 6:13). All believers have their 'day of evil', when faith is tried to the limits and Satan seems to be on our back, taunting, mocking, accusing and directing his fiery missiles at us. These are days when we find ourselves in a tight corner, being pressurised on every side; days when the warfare is carried over into our homes and

families, in the form of rebellious teenagers or handling
problems in the marriage; and particularly when the battle
enters the citadel of our own hearts and minds, and Satan
makes us question the reality of our faith and even doubt our
own salvation.

But in all this God will not supersede our own personal
efforts. He infuses courage and strength into us by promising, as he did to Joshua, that he will 'never leave . . . nor forsake' us. But he will not fight the battle in our place. In some
quarters there is the mistaken idea that God will fight our
battles and we have only to enjoy the fruits of his victory.
That is not scriptural teaching as I understand it. If we want
to be strong and courageous and victorious in our Christian
faith, then we have to work at it, always reminding ourselves
that God in Christ is always there in the thick of the battle,
and that he will never leave us nor forsake us.

## The study of God's Word

God did more than exhort Joshua to be strong and courageous. He also gave him some practical advice by telling him
to read and study his Word, because the battles ahead would
be governed and regulated by its truths and teachings.

> Do not let this Book of the Law depart from your mouth;
> meditate on it day and night, so that you may be careful to
> do everything written in it. Then you will be prosperous
> and successful (Joshua 1:8).

The application of that to ourselves is almost self-evident. If
we are to fight the Lord's battle in this life and overcome the
world, the flesh and the devil, then we can only do it in God's
way, and that means knowing the ground rules enshrined in

the Scriptures. Like Joshua, we need to read and meditate on God's Word (the Bible), familiarising ourselves with it and digging into its riches. I remember listening to a lecture by Dr Jim Packer in which he mentioned that one of his favourite texts was the words of the Psalmist: 'Your word is a lamp to my feet and a light for my path' (Psalm 119:105). He explained that the only time we need a light or lamp is when we are in the dark, illustrating his point with a reference to the black-out period during the Second World War, when there were no street lights in our towns and cities because of enemy aircraft, and people could only pick their way through the darkness with the help of a lamp or torch. But his main point was that the torch only gave a small circle of light immediately in front of one's feet, and the surrounding area remained in darkness. And that is the function of God's Word in the Scriptures. Through meditating on it we may not get the answers to all our questions; but there is always light enough to see our way through this dark world of confusion and sin.

We can say, therefore, that we need to meditate upon and study God's Word for two essential reasons. First, because of its inspirational value. It is God speaking to us; therefore the more we meditate on it, the more real God becomes to us. Through the gospel recorded in the Scriptures the Lord Jesus feeds our souls. In the battle with sin and temptation, and when our circumstances begin to wear us down, God's Word bolsters our confidence and lifts our spirits. Second, we meditate upon God's Word in order to inform our minds concerning the great doctrines of our faith and to apply its principles as a guide to life and conduct. If we don't know our Bibles, how can we witness to others concerning the things of God and the salvation to be found only in the Lord Jesus Christ? As to our conduct, the Bible is meant to help us in all the practical aspects of life. It enables us to settle difficult questions of conscience, it gives teaching on marriage and the family, on the management of money, on the conduct of relationships, on the use of our time and on a right attitude to daily work. In short, the Bible is a 'living' word, not only in the sense that in it the living God himself speaks to us, but also in the sense that it is a book that is meant to be lived. If we spent more time meditating on it, many of us would cope with the pressures of life in the modern world far better than we do.

# 9
# Caleb
## a man of conviction and courage

*Read Numbers 13:14 and Joshua 14:6-15*

The story of Caleb, the friend and contemporary of Joshua, has a peculiar fascination attaching to it, mainly because he embodies in his character those qualities which generally win respect from others even if they do not possess them themselves. He was a man of courage, conviction, faithfulness and sincerity. Of special interest is the fact that we are introduced to him at the age of forty, and take our leave of him when he is eighty-five and still showing the same qualities of character.

> I was forty years old when Moses the servant of the LORD sent me from Kadesh Barnea to explore the land . . . So here I am today, eighty-five years old! I am still as strong today as the day Moses sent me out; I'm just as vigorous to go out to battle now as I was then (Joshua 14:7,10,11).

## The courage of conviction

Caleb's story begins when he is chosen, along with Joshua, as one of the twelve spies Moses sent out to reconnoitre the land of Canaan.

> The LORD said to Moses, 'Send some men to explore the land of Canaan, which I am giving to the Israelites. From

each ancestral tribe send one of its leaders . . . from the
tribe of Judah, Caleb son of Jephunneh' (Numbers 13:1,6).

Moses gave them definite instructions about what to look
for, and at the end of forty days of exploration they returned
with their report, bringing with them evidence of the land's
fertility (vv.17-25). It is at this point that Caleb emerges as a
man with the courage of his convictions. Ten of the spies
gave a very damaging and discouraging report.

> They gave Moses this account: 'We went into the land to
> which you sent us, and it does flow with milk and honey!
> . . . But the people who live there are powerful, and the
> cities are fortified and very large. We even saw descen-
> dants of Anak there.' . . . Then Caleb silenced the people
> before Moses and said, 'We should go up and take posses-
> sion of the land, for we can certainly do it.' But the men
> who had gone up with him said, 'We can't attack those
> people; they are stronger than we are.' And they spread
> among the Israelites a bad report about the land they had
> explored. They said, 'The land we explored devours those
> living in it. All the people we saw there are of great size . . .
> We seemed like grasshoppers in our own eyes, and we
> looked the same to them' (vv.27-33).

Caleb must have been very unpopular with his fellow
spies for his straight speaking, and for taking what they
would consider the 'hard line'. But he spoke as his heart and
conscience led him and was not to be put off because the
others disagreed. He was a man who had the courage of his
convictions. He confirms this when he recalls the incident
before Joshua forty-five years later.

> I was forty years old when Moses the servant of the LORD
> sent me from Kadesh Barnea to explore the land. And I

brought him back a report according to my convictions, but my brothers who went up with me made the hearts of the people sink (Joshua 14:7,8).

There are times when all of us, as believers, are tempted to put expediency before personal convictions. Take a young Christian boy or girl leaving home for the first time to go to college or university. Previously they have spent most of their time in the company of other young Christians in their local church sharing the same spiritual outlook. But now suddenly they are in a totally secular environment, where the views expressed and the approach to life cut right across Christian thinking and behaviour. Do they speak up and make clear their own convictions concerning their salvation in Christ and why they refuse to go along with the lifestyle and values of their peers? It takes great courage to do that when you are a young person and you know how unpopular it can make you, even bringing down the ridicule of others upon you. But that is the kind of courage God looks for among his people today, even from young Christians. Daniel showed that firmness of conviction in the matter of the king's food, and he was only sixteen or seventeen at the time (Daniel 1:8). But as we know, God honoured him for his courage in the long run.

Preachers of the gospel also need the courage of conviction when it comes to exercising their ministry. It is tempting when engaging in a regular pulpit ministry to major on 'popular' preaching, dealing only with those subjects that are comforting and pleasing to the members of the congregation. But as preachers and teachers of the Word of God our task is to unfold the whole of the Scriptures to the people, so that we cover all the great truths and doctrines of God. When taking his leave of the Ephesian elders Paul reminded them that he had done just that. 'You know that I have not hesitated to preach anything that would be helpful to you but have taught you publicly and from house to house' (Acts 20:20). He was not selective in his ministry. He did not present those aspects of the gospel that were agreeable to them and keep quiet about the things that were unpopular. He declared the full counsel of God and kept back nothing that was profitable for their spiritual lives. Spurgeon on one occasion spoke disparagingly of those preachers who use biblical texts like coat hangers on which to hang a few spiritual platitudes. The preacher with the courage of the conviction that he must proclaim 'the *whole* will of God' (v.27) will never do that.

## The refusal to be discouraged

Caleb's fellow spies were not only discouraged and demoralised in themselves by what they saw in Canaan, but they conveyed their sense of discouragement to the rest of the people.

> 'All the people we saw there are of great size . . . We seemed like grasshoppers in our own eyes, and we looked the same to them.' That night all the people of the community raised their voices and wept aloud (Numbers 13:32–14:1)

They were totally demoralised. In the warfare of the Spirit with the forces of evil in the world it is bad enough that believers should seem as insignificant as grasshoppers in the eyes of others, but when we seem as grasshoppers 'in our own eyes' we are in a sorry state indeed. It means we have had all the stuffing knocked out of us and have lost sight of who and what we are.

Caleb on the other hand, along with Joshua, took an entirely different line and refused to be discouraged in the face of the enemy:

Joshua son of Nun and Caleb son of Jephunneh, who were among those who had explored the land, tore their clothes and said to the entire Israelite assembly, 'The land we passed through and explored is exceedingly good. If the LORD is pleased with us, he will lead us into that land, a land flowing with milk and honey, and will give it to us. Only do not rebel against the LORD. And do not be afraid of the people of the land, because we will swallow them up. Their protection is gone, but the LORD is with us. Do not be afraid of them' (14:6-9).

What a tremendous affirmation of triumphant faith that is—'we will swallow them up'! Forty-five years later, when claiming his inheritance from Joshua, he is still the same undaunted Caleb who refuses to be discouraged, however dark the situation or however powerful are the enemies of God's people.

Now give me this hill country that the LORD promised me that day. You yourself heard then that the Anakites were there and their cities were large and fortified, but, the LORD helping me, I will drive them out just as he said (Joshua 14:12).

This man never gives up, does he?

I dare say many of us, especially those in the work of ministry, have wanted to give up at times because of the godlessness of the age and the half-heartedness in spiritual matters one encounters even in the church itself. But have things ever been any different in the work of God? Remember Paul's words? 'Therefore, since through God's mercy we have this ministry, we do not lose heart' (2 Corinthians 4:1). He is surely implying that the temptation to lose heart and

become discouraged was something he and his fellow workers had to struggle with. For it is not wrong to be tempted
with feelings of discouragement; it is only wrong when, as
with all temptation, we give in to it and allow a defeatist
spirit to lay hold of us. In the above passage from 2 Corinthians Paul goes on to make that very point. 'We are hard
pressed on every side, but not crushed; perplexed, but not in
despair; persecuted, but not abandoned; struck down, but
not destroyed' (vv.8-9). Christians are under great pressure
today, but it should serve only to drive us back upon God,
not to bring us to defeat.

## The reward of faithfulness

Caleb may have been in a minority at one time, with every
man's hand against him to such an extent that, with Moses,
Aaron and Joshua, he was in danger of being stoned to death
(Numbers 14:10); but God honoured him in the long run and
rewarded him for his faithfulness. 'But because my servant
Caleb has a different spirit and follows me wholeheartedly, I
will bring him into the land he went to, and his descendants
will inherit it' (v.24). Later, when Caleb was an old man,
Joshua fulfilled that promise. 'Then Joshua blessed Caleb
son of Jephunneh and gave him Hebron as his inheritance'
(Joshua 14:13).

Everywhere in the Bible there is this teaching that God
rewards the faithfulness of his servants. This seems to trouble
some people: any talk of rewards, they feel, smacks of the
mercenary mind. But the Lord Jesus had a great deal to say
about rewards in his Sermon on the Mount. He says that
when we are under the stress of persecution we are to 'Rejoice and be glad, because great is your reward in heaven'
(Matthew 5:12). When we give to others, and when we pray,

it must be done in secret, and 'Then your Father, who sees what is done in secret, will reward you' (6:4,6). Not only is the idea of reward encouraged but we are actively to pursue it. 'Do not store up for yourselves treasures on earth, where moth and rust destroy, and where thieves break in and steal. But store up for yourselves treasures in heaven . . .' (vv.19-20). Paul also teaches the promise of rewards over and above the salvation that is ours in Christ. 'For we must all appear before the judgment seat of Christ, that each one may receive what is due to him for the things done while in the body, whether good or bad' (2 Corinthians 5:10).

In living our Christian lives here below, therefore, we are not to be influenced by the thought of rewards in terms of material prosperity and the praises of our fellow men, but by the thought of eternal reward in heaven and being in the presence of God. This is our inheritance, which we shall enter into one day, just as Caleb entered into his. We are a people destined for heaven because God has promised it to us in Christ.

> In my Father's house are many rooms; if it were not so, I would have told you. I am going there to prepare a place for you. And if I go and prepare a place for you, I will come back and take you to be with me that you also may be where I am (John 14:2,3).

As God's people we are going home (see 2 Corinthians 5:8) to claim our inheritance, which, as Peter says, 'can never perish, spoil or fade—kept in heaven for you' (1 Peter 1:4).

# 10
# Gideon
### farmer's boy to mighty warrior

*Read Judges 6*

Gideon didn't actually own the farm on which he worked; it belonged to his father Joash the Abiezrite and was situated in the village of Ophrah in central Palestine. They were hard times for settled farmers, because for several years marauding bands of Midianite tribesmen would regularly sweep across the land destroying everything in sight.

> Whenever the Israelites planted their crops, the Midianites . . . invaded the country. They . . . ruined the crops . . . and did not spare a living thing for Israel, neither sheep nor cattle nor donkeys . . . Midian so impoverished the Israelites that they cried out to the LORD for help (Judges 6:3-6).

That was the state of things when Gideon, who was busy at his work, was surprised one day by an amazing visitor:

> The angel of the LORD came and sat down under the oak in Ophrah that belonged to Joash the Abiezrite, where his son Gideon was threshing wheat in a winepress to keep it from the Midianites (v.11).

## The angel visitor

For some people this opening to the story of Gideon becomes an immediate sticking point. They find it difficult to believe that angels come to earth, especially when they look and act just like any ordinary human being. This one sat down under a tree and began chatting to Gideon as he was busy threshing wheat. 'When the angel of the LORD appeared to Gideon, he said, "The LORD is with you, mighty warrior."' (Judges 6:12). Even Gideon himself found it hard to believe that he was actually talking to a divine being until later in the story (v.22). Do we believe in angels? More than that, do we believe that they come to earth in human form as God's messengers? In the story of Abraham, he was visited by three angels in human form who told him of the coming birth of Isaac and the coming judgment on Sodom (Genesis 18). Moreover, the writer of the letter to the Hebrews tells us we are to expect such surprise visits from angels (Hebrews 13:2).

When you reflect on it, it seems no more difficult to accept that angels appear in human form than it is to accept the appearance of the Lord Jesus after his resurrection. He too ate and drank with his disciples to show them that he was no insubstantial spirit. And yet his body was different because it was a glorified body, and he was able to appear to the disciples in the upper room even when the doors were locked (John 20:19). The Lord Jesus also said that we too one day 'will be like the angels in heaven' (Matthew 22:30). That means at least two things:

a) We shall be like the angels in beauty and strength, with bodies no longer subject to disease and pain as they are now.

b) We shall be like the angels in purity and holiness, living in perfect harmony with God. What a glorious prospect that is for the Christian!

## Alone with God

When Gideon received his message from God he was alone, down in the winepress carrying out his daily work. In the

Bible that is often a characteristic of God's appearances or revelations to men. In many of the meetings of God with Abraham he was alone (see e.g. Genesis 15:12-16). Jacob was alone on the mountainside at Bethel when God spoke to him (Genesis 28). Moses too was alone on the mountainside when God spoke to him out of the burning bush (Exodus 3). Joshua was alone when the Lord's angel appeared to him before the battle of Jericho (Joshua 5:13). Zechariah was alone in the temple when the angel Gabriel appeared to him to announce the coming birth of John the Baptist (Luke 1:11). Joseph was alone when the angel appeared and told him of the divine conception of the Lord Jesus (Matthew 1:20).

I find all these instances, and there are many others, highly significant from the spiritual standpoint of meeting with God. We sometimes need to be alone with our own thoughts and meditations in order that God might get through to us more clearly. We can be so involved with the encumbering concerns of daily life that God rarely gets our full attention in order to speak with us. I was visiting a Christian brother in hospital recently and he said to me: 'You know, being in this room on my own all this time, I've been doing a lot of serious thinking about my Christian life.' I could well believe it. Sometimes, if we can't or won't get the time to be alone with God, he will force it upon us by laying us low so that we get the time, in the middle of the busyness of life, to meditate and think and in general to open ourselves up to God in ways we would not otherwise do.

Ours is an activist society, and we can all get caught up in it to the extent that we rarely get time to be alone with God. Even our Christian 'busyness' and involvement in church work can be a hindrance in this regard. There is a balance to be struck between action for God and meditation upon God, and we do not always get it right.

## Self-image

The angel's first words to Gideon were quite remarkable: 'The LORD is with you, mighty warrior' (Judges 6:12). Gideon might have looked up out of the winepress and said something like, 'Who, me? Mighty warrior? You're wrong, you know.' After all, he was a farmer, not a fighter; more used to handling the plough than the sword. His threshing wheat in a winepress, which was a cistern hewn out of the rock, shows how nervous he was of the Midianites. He just wasn't the hero type, and he certainly didn't think of himself as a great warrior and leader. And yet God always knows his man and is never wrong. It is evident that Gideon couldn't understand why God should choose him as the national deliverer. '"But LORD," Gideon asked, "how can I save Israel? My clan is the weakest in Manasseh and I am the least of my family"' (v.15). He clearly had a very low self-image.

This question of self-image is a delicate one and we need to get the balance right. On the one hand, we must be humble and not have any inflated ideas of our own ability. As Paul wisely says: 'If anyone thinks he is something when he is nothing, he deceives himself' (Galatians 6:3). There are folk like that, whose self-image rests on an illusion: they think they are more competent than they really are. In fairness to Gideon, his self-image may have been the mark of a humble heart. He knew himself to be a farmer and he had no illusions about being anything else. That has often been the mark of the great servants of God. Moses said to God: 'Who am I, that I should go to Pharaoh and bring the Israelites out of Egypt?' (Exodus 3:11). And Jeremiah, when called to be a prophet and spokesman for God, said: 'Ah, Sovereign LORD, I do not know how to speak; I am only a child' (Jeremiah 1:6).

That is one side of the matter. But we must also be careful

that our self-image is not so low that we become spiritually
paralysed where God's service is concerned and ask ourselves in effect: 'How can God use me? What have I to offer?
I don't have any special gift or potential.' And so we adopt a
totally negative attitude. There was something of that about
Gideon, and God had to speak very firmly to him; he was to
use whatever gifts and strength he had and not be so negative.

> The LORD turned to him and said, 'Go in the strength you
> have and save Israel out of Midian's hand. Am I not send-
> ing you? . . . I will be with you, and you will strike down
> all the Midianites together' (Judges 6:14,16).

Where the work of the gospel is concerned, if we wait until
we have everything before we do anything, we shall end up
by doing nothing.

## Scepticism

But Gideon was still not wholly convinced that he was the
right man for the job, and in any case he had already expressed his deep scepticism when the angel had said that the
Lord was with him and with his people Israel.

> 'But sir,' Gideon replied, 'if the LORD is with us, why has all
> this happened to us? Where are all his wonders that our
> fathers told us about when they said, "Did not the LORD
> bring us up out of Egypt?" But now the LORD has aban-
> doned us and put us into the hand of Midian' (Judges 6:13).

We can understand how he felt. Haven't we been equally
sceptical when, like Gideon, we read about the great revivals
God brought about in the past, with thousands being added
to the churches, and then look at the spiritual situation in the
country today and ask ourselves: Where is God now? Why
aren't we seeing his power at work today? Has he abandoned

us and permanently withdrawn his blessing from us? I think there are two things we should keep in mind regarding this state of affairs.

(a) First, it is true that we are living in the day of 'small things' on the spiritual scene. God is indeed withholding his blessing from us in a substantial measure, as is evident from the poor state of so many of our churches. But it cannot be that God has abandoned his people or forsaken his Church. That would be a downright denial of Jesus' promise when he said: 'I will build my church' (Matthew 16:18). We must stand on that and believe that when the time is right God will visit us again in the power of the Spirit and deliver his Church and people from the awful malaise that has fallen on us, just as he delivered Israel from the oppression of Midian through Gideon himself.

(b) Second, we must never forget that God is always working and saving people, even when we do not see the great blessing that comes with revival. Sometimes we can be guilty of praying and waiting for revival and a great out-pouring of the Spirit, whilst at the same time forgetting that there is a work to be done here and now. 'The day of small things' (Zechariah 4:10) it may be, but the gospel still has to be preached, souls still need saving, the missionary work of the Church still has to go forward, and prayers and intercessions still have to be made. So let us get on with it and use, to the best of our ability, the resources we already have. God says to us as he did to Gideon: 'Go in the strength you have . . . Am I not sending you?'

## Confirmation

Like Jephthah and Samson, who were of a similar mould, Gideon is described in Hebrews 11:32 as a man of faith alongside such great names as Abel, Enoch, Noah, Abraham and Moses. But the truth is that Gideon didn't come to strong faith all at once. It took a little time. God was very gentle and understanding with him and brought him gradually to spiritual maturity. That is what lay behind his request for confirmation of his calling to be the deliverer of God's people. He still found it hard to convince himself that he was the 'mighty warrior' the angel said he was.

> Gideon replied, 'If now I have found favour in your eyes, give me a sign that it is really you talking to me. Please do not go away until I come back and bring my offering and set it before you' . . . With the tip of the staff . . . the angel of the LORD touched the meat and the unleavened bread. Fire flared from the rock, consuming the meat and the bread . . . [Gideon] exclaimed . . . 'I have seen the angel of the LORD face to face!' (Judges 6:17-18, 21,22).

Later, Gideon again asks God for a sign of confirmation.

> Gideon said to God, 'If you will save Israel by my hand . . . look, I will place a wool fleece on the threshing-floor. If there is dew only on the fleece and all the ground is dry, then I will know that you will save Israel' . . . Gideon rose early the next day; he squeezed the fleece and wrung out the dew . . . Then Gideon said to God, 'Do not be angry with me . . . This time make the fleece dry and the ground covered with dew.' That night God did so (vv.36-40).

So he got his confirmation and his faith was made that little bit stronger. It is like that with us at times. We too want the certainty that it really is God who is calling us and giving us a work to do, and that it is not just our own subjective feelings that are in play. That is a perfectly natural and worthy desire. Our faith can indeed be weak, especially at the outset of our Christian life, and God is very willing to give us confirmation in one way or another.

But let us not forget that asking for a sign is really an indication of spiritual immaturity, and our aim should be to 'walk by faith and not by sight'. In Matthew's Gospel we have a quotation from Isaiah describing the Servant of the Lord which is a great encouragement to all whose faith is weak and faltering: 'A bruised reed he will not break, and a smouldering wick he will not snuff out' (12:20). Just as the reed can hardly stand and the light is reduced to a flicker, so a Christian may be weak and his faith a mere spark; but the Lord Jesus treats neither with contempt. With his own power and love he strengthens the bruised reed and fans the spark of faith into a flame.

# 11
# Gideon
## and God's selection

*Read Judges 7*

Convinced that God was now with him, Gideon mus-
tered an army of thirty-two thousand (Judges 7:3)
with which to fight the Midianites. This was a small
enough number compared with the vast army of Midian
described as 'thick as locusts. Their camels could no more be
counted than the sand on the seashore' (Judges 7:12). But
imagine Gideon's dismay when God through a process of
selection reduced his army to a mere three hundred.

> The LORD said to Gideon, 'You have too many men for me
> to deliver Midian'. . . So twenty-two thousand men left,
> while ten thousand remained. But the LORD said to Gideon,
> 'There are still too many men. Take them down to the
> water, and I will sift them out for you there' . . . The LORD
> said . . . 'With the three hundred men that lapped I will
> save you and give you the Midianites into your hands'
> (Judges 7:2-4,7).

What was the significance of this selection process and
what are we meant to learn from it?

## A biblical principle

This process of selecting, sifting and choosing by God is a
theme that runs right through the Bible. Abraham was a man

right at the centre of God's choice when he selected and
called him out of the pagan culture of Ur of the Chaldeans
(Genesis 12:1-3). Why him? We don't know; it was God's
sovereign choice. Why did God select a crowd of Hebrew
slaves in Egypt to become his chosen people and the instrument of his purposes in the world? We don't know; that too
must be put down to God's sovereign choice.

And when we come to the important matter of our salvation, the same process of selection and choice is at work.
The Lord Jesus said to his disciples: 'You did not choose me,
but I chose you' (John 15:16). Then there are those remarkable words in Matthew 22:14, 'For many are invited, but few
are chosen.' Many receive the invitation of the gospel, but
only a few respond to it by God's grace. Paul states this principle of God's choice even more forcefully when he says:

> In him we were also chosen, having been predestined
> according to the plan of him who works out everything in
> conformity with the purpose of his will, in order that we,
> who were the first to hope in Christ, might be for the
> praise of his glory (Ephesians 1:11-12).

We may not fully understand this principle of God's selection, but it certainly humbles us when we know that we are
at the centre of God's choice. It is incredible that without any
merit on our part God should have chosen us 'before the
creation of the world' (Ephesians 1:4) to receive salvation
through the Lord Jesus Christ.

## God delivers

By the selection process God wanted Gideon and the nation
to be in no doubt whatever that deliverance from the Midianites would be through his power alone and not through

the nation's fighting efficiency or Gideon's generalship—
'Israel may not boast against me that her own strength has
saved her' (Judges 7:2). By winning a victory with a mere
three hundred men it would be seen that the power and the
glory were God's alone.

This principle that God gets all the glory underlies all our
work for him, as Paul makes clear: 'But God chose the foolish
things of the world to shame the wise; God chose the weak
things of the world to shame the strong. He chose the lowly
things of this world and the despised things—and the things
that are not—to nullify the things that are, so that no one
may boast before him' (1 Corinthians 1:27-29). How often in
the history of the Church have the greatest victories for
God's kingdom been accomplished through the weakest
instruments!

Take the first disciples; they could hardly be described as
men of great intellect and influence, and yet they were the
instruments God used to sweep through the Roman empire
with the message of salvation. Think of John Bunyan, without formal schooling or education, and yet God used him to
write *Pilgrim's Progress*, which has influenced many generations. William Carey was a cobbler, but became the father of
modern missions. William Booth began as a pawnbroker's
assistant, but through his Salvation Army God used him as a
social force to march through the world in the name of the
Lord Jesus. When a reporter covering Moody's campaigns
wrote, 'I can see nothing in Moody to account for this spiritual success and marvellous work,' the evangelist said: 'That
is the secret of my success; there's nothing of me in it; it is the
power of God, and the victory is God's, not mine.'

All this means that there is no room in God's work for personal praise or boasting, for the power and glory are God's
alone. This is especially true in the work of salvation. We can

no more save or deliver ourselves from the dominion of sin and the power of darkness than Gideon could deliver Israel from the power of Midian with a mere three hundred men. God alone can save us through the power of the Holy Spirit. 'For it is by grace you have been saved, through faith—and this not from yourselves, it is the gift of God—not by works, so that no one can boast' (Ephesians 2:8-9).

## Faith tested

The selection process was also a test of Gideon's faith. Would he dare do battle against superior forces with such an inadequate army? It was a mighty challenge. This testing of faith in the challenges and trials of life is one of the main themes of the Bible. James Philip in his Bible Notes on Judges gives a pertinent quote from C. S. Lewis on this subject of the trial of faith.

> God has not been trying an experiment on my faith or love in order to find out their quality. He knew it already. It was I who didn't. In this trial, he makes me occupy the dock, the witness-box and the bench all at once. He always knew that my temple was a house of cards. His only way of making me realise the fact was to knock it down.

When God tries our faith, therefore, by allowing us to become casualties in the warfare of life through sickness, trouble or disappointment, it is not because he wants to know how weak our faith is since he knows that already. It is we who need that information in order to do something about our faith if and when it lets us down. That is why James says, 'Consider it pure joy, my brothers, whenever you face trials of many kinds, because you know that the testing of your faith develops perseverance' (James 1:2-3).

God doesn't want us to adopt a 'victim' mentality in the face of life's difficulties, for that can only lead to self-pity, which is a destructive emotion. Rather he wants us to adopt a more positive approach, by recognising that in our exposure to the cutting edge of life in all its challenges we can prove to ourselves that our faith in God's keeping grace is not a fantasy and delusion.

## Numbers count for nothing with God

Why is it that even as Christians we are so impressed with numbers and size? We are forever counting heads. The bigger the congregation, the more confident we are that God is present among us. If the number of new members joining a church in a year is not in double figures, we conclude that not much of spiritual value has been achieved. The figure of three hundred to which God reduced Gideon's army was purely arbitrary. It could have been two hundred and fifty or seventy-five or five thousand—it wouldn't have mattered. All God wanted to do was to teach Gideon that numbers were irrelevant where he is concerned. It is a lesson to us not to confine or limit God to our human way of thinking.

Andrew said to Jesus at the feeding of the five thousand: 'Here is a boy with five small barley loaves and two small fish, but how far will they go among so many?' (John 6:9). He too was thinking only of size and numbers. But the Lord Jesus showed him how wrong he was. We do the same thing when it comes to time. We tend to imprison God within our time frame as though he has to work according to the calendar. Peter warned that people would say: 'Where is this "coming" he promised? Ever since our fathers died, everything goes on as it has since the beginning of creation' (2 Peter 3:4). We get frustrated and impatient when we do not see things happening in the Christian life as quickly as we wish, and we would like to hurry God up a bit. But although God works within time, he is not governed by time. Hence Peter reminds us: 'do not forget this one thing, dear friends: With the Lord a day is like a thousand years, and a thousand years are like a day' (2 Peter 3:8).

So let us learn the lesson that, in God's world, what is accomplished does not depend in the final analysis upon the time factor, numbers, size, resources or any of these things, since they are all irrelevant to God and he can use them or ignore them as he pleases. We need to pay attention to these things, but always we must let God be God. 'Not by might nor by power, but by my Spirit, says the LORD Almighty' (Zechariah 4:6).

Two other brief points arise out of this chapter.

## God prepares the way

At God's bidding Gideon reconnoitred the Midian camp and heard one of the men telling a fellow soldier of a dream he had had during the night.

> 'I had a dream . . . A round loaf of barley bread came tumbling into the Midianite camp. It struck a tent with such force that the tent overturned and collapsed.' His friend responded, 'This can be nothing other than the sword of Gideon . . . God has given the Midianites and the whole camp into his hands' (Judges 7:13-14).

Clearly this teaches us that in his work God often prepares the way for his servants. News of the miraculous way God had raised up Gideon to be Israel's leader had got through to the Midianites, and the psychological pressure was building up. It was just the assurance Gideon needed that God was preparing the way for victory.

God often does that. Moses must have wondered how he
would lead the vast company of Israel through the wilderness, but God told him he would prepare the way in the
pillar of cloud by day and the pillar of fire by night. When
Philip the evangelist was led to the Gaza road (Acts 8), God
had already prepared the heart of the Ethiopian eunuch to
receive the gospel. God used the ministry of John the Baptist
to prepare the way for the coming of Christ. Whenever we
engage on a work of God, we must remind ourselves that
God has already gone before preparing the way. This is
especially true in preaching and evangelisation. It is not a
hit-and-miss affair whether people are receptive to our message. God by his Spirit prepares people's hearts. And let us
not forget that God has also prepared the way when death
meets us at the last. The Lord Jesus said of his ascension into
heaven, 'I am going there to prepare a place for you' (John
14:2).

## The Lord's battle

Although Gideon, through the dream he had heard, was
confident that God would give the victory in battle, he
nevertheless worked out his own strategy for the way in
which that battle would be won. The battle was the Lord's,
but Gideon still had his own part to play. The three hundred
men were divided into companies of one hundred, and each
man was given a trumpet and an earthenware pitcher containing a lighted torch. Under cover of darkness, when the
camp was asleep, each man on a given signal blew the trumpet and smashed the pitcher so that the light blazed out, and
shouted the battle cry, 'For the LORD and for Gideon'. The
result was devastating: what with the noise and confusion,
blazing lights and trumpet blasts, the Midianites were thrown

into total panic, thinking they were being attacked by a huge army, and they fled in disarray. Today it might be called 'psychological warfare'. Be that as it may, it was both clever and successful and was Gideon's own contribution to overcoming the enemy.

The New Testament makes it clear that as believers we are engaged in a lasting warfare with the powers of evil and darkness in this world. 'For our struggle is not against flesh and blood, but against the rulers, against the authorities, against the powers of this dark world and against the spiritual forces of evil in the heavenly realms' (Ephesians 6:12). And whilst we know that the ultimate victory is with God and his Son, the battle is ours in the sense that we simply cannot relax in God's victory. God provides the armour, but we have to put it on: '. . . be strong in the Lord and in his mighty power. Put on the full armour of God so that you can take your stand against the devil's schemes' (Ephesians 6:10,11). And when Satan launches his attack in the 'evil day', directing his 'flaming arrows' at us, we sometimes have to work out our own strategy as to how to defeat him. Do we need to be stronger in our prayer life, in worship and the reading of God's Word? Are there places and people we should avoid because they are a snare to us?

There are occasions when God acts independently of us. But for the most part God uses our faith, our trust, our common sense and wisdom, our intelligence and gifts and ideas in the warfare of the Spirit and in the furtherance of his kingdom in the world. Satan has his strategy; he is always scheming and planning to retain his grip on the hearts of men and women and to undermine the faith of God's people. We, with God's help, must outwit, outplan and outflank him in every way we can, always keeping in mind that the battle is the Lord's, and every victory won is his alone.

## Gideon's failure

When we move into chapter eight the story of Gideon ends on a sad note. So grateful were the people for his leadership that they invited him to become their king and establish a hereditary monarchy, but he refused and said, 'The LORD will rule over you' (v.23). He was wise to refuse, for he could see that the nation was not yet ready for the institution of monarchy. But then he acted very unwisely and wilfully in asking for a share of the plunder and using it for sinful purposes. 'Gideon made the gold into an ephod, which he placed in Ophrah, his town. All Israel prostituted themselves by worshipping it there, and it became a snare to Gideon and his family' (Judges 8:27). In the time of adversity and trial Gideon was courageous and faithful, but in the final years of prosperity he was weak and faithless. The gold was made into a shrine for idolatrous worship, and Gideon's spiritual life began to go downhill; spiritually speaking, he went to seed.

Is that a warning to us? Does it help to explain why believers in countries where there is persecution are so alive and positive in their faith, while in the prosperity and materialism of the West they are so often lukewarm and apathetic? It doesn't have to be like that, not if we keep material prosperity in its proper place. By all means let us enjoy the good things of this world and the happiness and pleasure they can bring, but let us never allow them to displace God from the central position in our lives.

# 12
# Deborah
## a mother in Israel

*Read Judges 4 and 5*

We have already considered Gideon, and in the next chapter we shall be considering Jephthah: these two of Israel's judges were strong, rough personalities during a dark period in the history of God's people. It comes as something of a surprise, therefore, suddenly to find a woman emerging as the nation's deliverer in the time of crisis. The background to Deborah's story is given in the opening verses.

> After Ehud died, the Israelites once again did evil in the eyes of the LORD. So the LORD sold them into the hands of Jabin, a king of Canaan, who reigned in Hazor. The commander of his army was Sisera, who lived in Harosheth Haggoyim. Because he had nine hundred iron chariots and had cruelly oppressed the Israelites for twenty years, they cried to the LORD for help (Judges 4:1-3).

The reference to nine hundred iron chariots signifies how advanced Jabin's forces were in terms of military equipment, and how desperate and hopeless the situation was in the eyes of the Israelites. In the light of this we are told that they 'cried to the LORD for help', and the help God gave them was in the person of a woman.

Deborah, a prophetess, the wife of Lappidoth, was leading Israel at that time. She held court under the Palm of Deborah between Ramah and Bethel in the hill country of Ephraim, and the Israelites came to her to have their disputes decided (Judges 4:4-5).

Although quite an ordinary woman in one sense, being a wife and mother, Deborah nevertheless was quite extraordinary in the part she played under God's hand on the stage of Israel's history. It is all the more intriguing, therefore, that in the roll-call of the great Old Testament heroes of the faith in Hebrews 11 the writer refers to Barak, who played a subsidiary role under Deborah, but makes no mention of Deborah herself, who was the woman of God's choice. In the description given in verse 4 we are told three things about Deborah.

## A prophetess

She exercised a prophetic gift. We looked at the meaning of the term 'prophetess' when dealing with the character of Miriam, and we saw that it meant a woman through whom God spoke his word. It did not necessarily include the gift of foretelling future events, but it meant essentially that both Miriam and Deborah were a voice for God in revealing his will and purpose for the people. It is significant in this regard that both have a song attributed to them following victory over God's enemies. The 'ode' or song of Deborah in chapter 5 was in all likelihood the expression of her prophetic gift, as it tells forth the acts of God.

On that day Deborah and Barak son of Abinoam sang this song: 'When the princes in Israel take the lead, when the people willingly offer themselves—praise the LORD! Hear this, you kings! Listen, you rulers! I will sing to the LORD, I

will sing; I will make music to the LORD, the God of Israel'
(Judges 5:1-3).

There then follows a recitation of God's activity in the victory over Jabin and his forces.

The prophetic gift, in the sense of telling forth the truths of
God already revealed in Scripture, is in principle open to any
Christian man or woman. God has ordained in his Word that
men should exercise it through the preaching ministry, but
there are also other ways. Like Deborah, some have the gift
of poetry, and this can be a very powerful instrument the
Spirit may use for the presentation of divine truth. One has
only to think of Charles Wesley and the nearly 9,000 hymns
he wrote, many of which have been so mightily used of God
in acts of worship and in proclaiming the way of salvation.

## A housewife and mother

We are told that Deborah was the wife of Lappidoth, of whom
we know nothing whatsoever. But in addition she describes
herself in her song as 'a mother in Israel' (5:7). For some
strange reason this phrase has come to mean, especially in
evangelical circles, something quite different from what
Deborah had in mind. It is generally used now to describe an
elderly godly woman, perhaps in the local church, who is of a
motherly disposition and is helpful and kind and faithful in
the Lord's work. But Deborah used it, so it would seem, in the
straightforward sense that she was a housewife with a family
to care for. Indeed the very point she makes in the song is that,
at a time when things were so bad in the country that people
couldn't walk the roads through fear of crime and violence
and normal village life had all but ceased, God had to call
upon an ordinary housewife and mother like herself because
there was no leader forthcoming from among the men.

In the days of Shamgar son of Anath, in the days of Jael, the roads were abandoned; travellers took to winding paths. Village life in Israel ceased, ceased until I, Deborah, arose, arose a mother in Israel (vv.6-7).

This point is reinforced in the opening part of our story when Deborah, under God's direction, commands Barak to take up the reins of leadership in delivering Israel from subjection to Jabin; but he refuses to do so unless she goes with him.

She sent for Barak son of Abinoam from Kedesh in Naphtali and said to him, 'The LORD, the God of Israel, commands you: 'Go, take with you ten thousand men of Naphtali and Zebulun and lead the way to Mount Tabor. I will lure Sisera, the commander of Jabin's army, with his chariots and his troops to the Kishon River and give him into your hands.' Barak said to her, 'If you go with me, I will go; but if you don't go with me, I won't go.' 'Very well,' Deborah said, 'I will go with you. But because of the way you are going about this, the honour will not be yours, for the LORD will hand Sisera over to a woman' (4:6-9).

All this raises a question with which we are only too familiar today in the life of the nation, the church and the family. Why do we see so many men failing to take responsibility in the leadership role, and so many women taking on that role themselves? We gain the impression from Deborah's song that she would have been only too happy if the leaders in Israel had accepted the responsibility. 'When the princes in Israel take the lead, when the people willingly offer themselves—praise the LORD!' (5:2).

The New Testament is clear in its teaching about the headship or leadership of the man in God's scheme of things. 'For the husband is the head of the wife as Christ is the head of the church' (Ephesians 5:23). Paul is here talking about Christian marriage, but the principle of the headship of the man applies in other directions. There are many church fellowships today where women are engaged in leading, guiding, teaching in Sunday school and, in general, giving direction and counsel; not that they particularly aspire to these positions, but because the men are either not available or, if they are, they simply opt out of leadership responsibility. The same is true of missionary work. The number of women taking up the challenge of overseas mission invariably outstrips that of men.

In many Christian families today far too many men have been influenced by the feminist unisex philosophy rather than by the teaching of the Word of God in this matter. Many pastors will relate the experience of wives complaining to them that their husbands are not giving the lead in the home, and that the responsibility of disciplining the children and taking family devotions has fallen on them, or else it isn't done. This abdication by men of the leadership role is something, I believe, most Christian women are deeply unhappy about, and they would much rather accept in practice the doctrine of the headship of the husband. For, make no mistake about it, God will not allow his cause to fail because the modern Baraks will not take it on. He will always raise up a Deborah.

## God uses the ordinary

We may also see in this picture of Deborah as a housewife and mother the way in which God uses ordinary people in his service and for the furtherance of the gospel. We can assume that Deborah was an able and gifted woman, and yet we are not told of any particular quality of leadership she

may have possessed or of any other position she may have
held as the reason why God chose her to be the leader of his
people. Indeed, her own words in her song—'until I, Deborah, arose, arose a mother in Israel'—suggest that she was
as surprised as anyone that God should have called her to be
Israel's deliverer in the time of crisis. But God often works in
that way, and it ought to be a great encouragement to those
of us who feel we are just 'ordinary' people without any special gift or talent. We recall the apostle's words:

> Brothers, think of what you were when you were called.
> Not many of you were wise by human standards; not
> many were influential; not many were of noble birth. But
> God chose the foolish things of the world to shame the
> wise; God chose the weak things of the world to shame the
> strong. He chose the lowly things of this world and the
> despised things—and the things that are not—to nullify
> the things that are, so that no one may boast before him
> (1 Corinthians 1:26-29).

That is often God's way, to choose the ordinary.

When Philip excitedly told Nathanael that he had met
with Jesus of Nazareth whom the prophets had foretold, he
replied with deep scepticism: 'Nazareth! Can anything good
come from there?' (John 1:46). He clearly felt that Nazareth
was far too ordinary and insignificant to make it the source
of any great blessing, let alone the home of God's own Son.
And we may be equally sceptical about ourselves when it
comes to the question of God using us in his service. 'Who,
me? I doubt it, I'm just an ordinary person with no particular
gift of any kind.' But that's just it. God does in fact use ordinary people like ourselves in so many ways. William Booth
began his working life in a pawnbroker's shop and Dwight L.

Moody as a shoe salesman, and look how God used them! We can't say that Deborah was or wasn't a highly gifted person. All we know from her own words is that she was an ordinary housewife and mother, and when God called her she responded to that call.

## Leader and judge

The third description we are given of Deborah is that she was a judge to whom the people came to have their problems and disputes settled. 'She held court under the Palm of Deborah between Ramah and Bethel in the hill country of Ephraim, and the Israelites came to her to have their disputes decided' (Judges 4:5). What kind of disputes she was called upon to deal with we cannot say, but in all probability, as she held her counselling sessions under the palm tree which she had made her headquarters, the people would come to her for help and advice on family and personal matters, as well as tribal differences. As one writer points out, it is particularly interesting that the 'first named judicial officer in the Bible should have been a woman, and a married woman at that'. When it comes to the other 'judges', we are told of their military prowess and fighting skills, their cunning and bravery; but only of Deborah is it said that she had this input into the daily lives of the people by helping them with their disputes and problems. One thing we can say with certainty therefore is that she could relate to other people; they found her to be a ready listener and a woman to whom they could talk.

This is not a gift given to everyone, if we can call it that, but those who have it can exercise a wonderful ministry at the spiritual level. Not even all pastors have it. A man may be a powerful preacher, a good organiser and leader; but he may lack the necessary pastoral 'touch' that makes his people feel they can share their burdens with him, knowing that he will give a sympathetic hearing and help them, if possible, with his wisdom and advice.

Today there is a tremendous emphasis upon 'counselling' in church life, and there are numerous books, lectures and training courses available for those who have the desire to become a 'professional' counsellor. Without minimising in any way the need for a person to be well informed and skilled in counselling techniques, it seems to me that there are other qualities which no amount of professional training can impart and which are essential in a person, if others are to gravitate towards them naturally for help and guidance when they need it. To begin with, they must have a love for people and be willing to accept them as they are, and not as they want them to be. Peter tells us, 'Above all, love each other deeply, because love covers over a multitude of sins' (1 Peter 4:8). This does not mean that we treat the sins of others lightly, but they will instinctively know that, in spite of their faults and foolishness, we love them and want to understand why they fell into sin. Peter is talking to ordinary Christians, so that it is open to any of us to be the kind of counsellor to whom others will turn in their distresses, finding in us someone who is prepared to listen.

# 13
# Jephthah
### the outlaw turned judge

*Read Judges 11*

Whe we study the characters of the Old Testament it may perplex us that God should have used in such a remarkable way men who were so awkward and difficult, and whose lives at times were downright sinful and violent. But we should never forget that the emphasis always lies, not on the characters themselves, but on the sovereign power of the God who worked through them. There is an old proverb which says, 'You can't make a silk purse out of a sow's ear'. But God is doing precisely that all the time. He takes an ugly distorted life like that of Jephthah and makes out of it something that has a certain glory and is productive in furthering his own purposes in history.

## A bad start in life

Jephthah's story opens with the description of his early upbringing:

> Jephthah the Gileadite was a mighty warrior. His father was Gilead; his mother was a prostitute. Gilead's wife also bore him sons, and when they were grown up, they drove Jephthah away. 'You are not going to get any inheritance in our family,' they said, 'because you are the son of another

woman.' So Jephthah fled from his brothers and settled in the land of Tob, where a group of adventurers gathered around him and followed him (Judges 11:1-3).

Clearly he didn't have a very promising start in life. The illegitimate son of a prostitute, hated by his half-brothers, he was deprived of his share in his father's inheritance and driven from home. The word 'fled' suggests that his very life was threatened. As a result of all this he took to the life of an adventurer in the wilderness of Tob, where he became a kind of outlaw-chief over a group of outcasts and misfits like himself and organised them into a disciplined body of fighting men. The amazing thing is that this was the man God chose to become the deliverer of the nation from the Ammonites and to be the judge over his people.

> So Jephthah went with the elders of Gilead, and the people made him head and commander over them. And he repeated all his words before the LORD in Mizpah' (Judges 11:11).

What took place at Mizpah was a kind of inauguration ceremony for Jephthah as head of state. Later we read: 'Then the Spirit of the LORD came upon Jephthah . . . and . . . he advanced against the Ammonites' (Judges 11:29).

We gather from all this that in the wilderness of Tob God made himself known to Jephthah, the gang-leader and outlaw, and transformed him into a man of faith. God then began moulding and shaping his character in readiness for the day when he would become the judge and deliverer of his people. In Hebrews 11 Jephthah appears alongside Gideon, David, Samuel and the prophets as a man of faith, and the writer then adds, 'whose weakness was turned to strength' (Hebrews 11:32-34). We are not meant to emulate the sinful weaknesses of men like Jephthah, therefore, but the strength of their faith.

Such transformations in human lives God is bringing about all the time. In his book *Men of Destiny* Peter Masters tells the story of Alves Reis who was regarded as the cleverest forger of his day; he defrauded the bank of Portugal of millions of pounds and brought down the government. He was sentenced to twenty-five years in prison and, during his time there, was sent a gospel tract by a missionary working in Portugal. His life was gloriously transformed by the power of God, and on his release in 1945 he became a lay preacher working with the evangelical churches in the Lisbon area.

Only God can take people like Alves Reis the forger, and Jephthah the outlaw-chief, and change them into the kind of people he wants them to be. He may be wanting to do that with us. But we must allow him to mould and shape our characters by his Spirit so as to become the kind of instrument he can use. The hymn puts it so well:

> Have Thine own way Lord,
>   Have Thine own way;
> Thou art the Potter,
>   I am the clay.
> Mould me and make me
>   After Thy will,
> While I am waiting
>   Yielded and still
>       Adelaide Addison Pollard 1862–1934

## Salvation by grace

Another thing we learn from Jephthah's background is that the knowledge and salvation of God does not depend, in the last analysis, on having a godly home and Christian upbringing—it is entirely the gift of God's grace. Unlike Samuel or David, who came from godly homes, there is nothing in Jephthah's home life to make us envy him. And yet, according to Hebrews 11, he comes down through history as a man commended for his faith. Where did he get it? It could only have been that God himself awoke faith in his heart.

That noted Bible commentator Matthew Henry says: 'Those who have most grace in their hearts cannot give grace to their children.' How true that is! We cannot guarantee the salvation of our children, however anxious we are to guard them against the ways of the world and to set them a godly example. The most we can do, and should do, is to remove every obstacle in the way of their salvation and to encourage them in the things of God. But in the end it is God himself, by his Spirit, who must work in their hearts to draw them to himself. But we must remind them of their own personal responsibility to seek the salvation that God desires to give them.

Furthermore, when we are involved in witness and evangelism, we must constantly remind ourselves that salvation is of the Lord and does not depend in the last resort upon our cogency in presenting the gospel, or on our ability to persuade people by our eloquence or force of argument. We must strive to explain the message clearly, but we must pray for the Holy Spirit to do his own convicting and saving work in bringing people to faith in the Lord Jesus Christ.

## When trouble comes

During his time in the wilderness of Tob, Jephthah's life must have been one of considerable loneliness and desolation. After all, he had been rejected by his own family and his own people. Nevertheless, when trouble came to Israel in the form of a threatened invasion by the pagan Ammonites, it was to the despised and rejected Jephthah that the elders of Israel turned. They had heard of his military prowess and qualities of leadership, and knew instinctively that he was the man to be the nation's saviour and deliverer.

> . . . the elders of Gilead went to get Jephthah from the land of Tob. 'Come,' they said, 'be our commander, so we can fight the Ammonites.' Jephthah said to them, 'Didn't you hate me and drive me from my father's house? Why do you come to me now, when you're in trouble?' The elders of Gilead said to him, 'Nevertheless, we are turning to you now; come with us to fight the Ammonites, and you will be our head over all who live in Gilead' (Judges 11:4-8).

The elders were made to feel very humble by Jephthah's reply; not that he was bitter  towards them in any way, since he readily forgave the past and went with them to Mizpah to take the oath to become leader and judge. Mizpah was an important sacred centre and, years later, was the place where Samuel crowned Saul the first king of Israel (1 Samuel 10:17-27). There are two things to be noted here.

(a) Although it took a considerable time, there came a day when God vindicated the faith of his servant Jephthah. And God always does that. He vindicates in his own time the faith of his servants and the truth of his cause in the world. We need to keep that in the forefront of our minds, because we are living at a time when, on the face of it, it seems that the forces of sin and evil, and the tyranny of lies and false-hood, are in control, and the way of God's truth and right-eousness in the gospel of the Lord Jesus is losing out. But that is not so. Or if it is, it can only be in the short term, since Satan and the powers of evil can never ultimately frustrate the purposes of God in history.

God's vindication of Jephthah's faith is a type of the vindication of the gospel of Jesus Christ. For our Lord too, like Jephthah, was hated and despised and rejected by the world, and when he was crucified on the cross of Calvary, it did indeed seem as if the forces of sin and darkness had triumphed. But then came the resurrection morning when God vindicated his truth in raising up the Lord Jesus and exalting him to the highest place. Let us hold to this, therefore, that God always vindicates his truth.

(b) We also see here that the people of Israel treated Jephthah in exactly the same way as many people treat God. It was only when they were faced with trouble and crisis that the elders turned to Jephthah—before then they had no time for him. In the same way, how often do people ignore God and turn their backs upon him, and then when crisis comes or trouble hits them, their thoughts begin to turn to spiritual concerns and the worship of God's house.

Again and again in times of national crisis the call goes out to the churches for prayer, or people are asked to spend a moment in prayerful silence, when for most of the time the life of our nation is totally devoid of any thought of God. Similarly how often have I, in common with other pastors when visiting in hospital, been asked by some patient facing an operation, 'Please say a prayer for me', when it is fairly certain that they have never given a thought to God in their lives before. God is very gracious and forgiving, and will not refuse to listen even when people turn to him only because they are in trouble. But that is not the way to know God's power in our lives. He wants us in Christ to know him personally and intimately as a loving heavenly Father and to share with him our joys as well as our troubles.

## Making vows and promises

We have said much about Jephthah's faith and courage, but now we have to deal with something he did which was absurd and foolish, something he ought never to have done. As we said at the outset, we are not meant to emulate the weaknesses of the characters of the Old Testament, but to learn from their faith and their strengths. Jephthah's foolishness lay in the rash vow he made to God prior to going into battle against the Ammonites.

> And Jephthah made a vow to the LORD: 'If you give the Ammonites into my hands, whatever comes out of the door of my house to meet me when I return in triumph from the Ammonites will be the LORD's, and I will sacrifice it as a burnt offering.' . . . When Jephthah returned to his home in Mizpah, who should come out to meet him but his daughter . . . She was an only child . . . When he saw her, he tore his clothes and cried, 'Oh! My daughter! You have made me miserable and wretched, because I have made a vow to the LORD that I cannot break' (Judges 11:30-31, 34-35).

It is still a debatable point among Bible students whether Jephthah did in fact offer up his daughter as a human sacrifice to God or kept her in a state of perpetual virginity. She herself requested: 'Give me two months to roam the hills and weep with my friends, because I will never marry' (Judges 11:37). But either way it was a vow he should never have made. In the first place, he had no need to bribe God with such a promise, since God had already raised him up for the purpose of defeating the Ammonites. Moreover, it was clearly stated in God's law that the Israelites were not to follow the evil practice of the surrounding pagans in offering up human sacrifice (Deuteronomy 18:9-10). Jephthah, through his rashness and stupidity, had got himself into an impossible position, one which would mean hurt and grief either way. If he kept the vow he lost his daughter. If he did not he would consider himself guilty before God.

In those far-off times, when men still had much to learn of the true nature of God, we may find it possible to excuse Jephthah, but this and other distasteful things are recorded in the Bible, says Paul, 'as examples and were written down as warnings for us, on whom the fulfilment of the ages has come' (1 Corinthians 10:11). So what do we learn from this incident?

Well, it is a warning to us not to make any promises or vows thoughtlessly, especially where God is concerned, since to do so can cause us endless trouble. One has only to think of the thousands of marriage vows broken every year and the deep guilt often associated with that. Then there are the vows or promises implicit when we become church members, or get baptised, or have our children dedicated or christened. All these can be made far too lightly, with many people not realising that God will hold them responsible for their fulfilment. The Lord Jesus had something to say about all this which we should take to heart.

> You have heard that it was said . . . 'Do not break your oath, but keep the oaths you have made to the Lord.' But I tell you, Do not swear at all . . . Simply let your 'Yes' be 'Yes,' and your 'No', 'No'; anything beyond this comes from the evil one (Matthew 5:33,34,37).

Our Lord is reminding us that we need to be very careful about the words we speak, since words are a reflection of our hearts. We must always speak the truth, meaning yes when we say yes and no when we say no. We are not to engage in double talk, in lies, deception or hypocrisy. All that belongs to the secular world, and he has laid down the principles in his Word whereby we are to direct our lives. We shall have to give an account to him one day, not only for the things we have done, but also for the words we have spoken.

# 15
# Samson
## a child of promise

*Read Judges 13*

More space is given to the account of Samson than to any other judge in Israel prior to the time of Samuel. His story extends from chapter 13 to 16 and presents us with a strange and complex personality. Samson is a mixture of spiritual anointing and failure in moral integrity, of manliness and childishness, of great physical strength and profound spiritual weakness. One cannot help wondering why God should have chosen such a man to be the leader of his people for a period of twenty years (Judges 15:20). But God is sovereign in all his ways, and his choice of such an instrument was deliberate and purposeful since Samson is mentioned among the great saints of the Old Testament in Hebrews 11. Moreover, in spite of his moral failure Samson was successful in fulfilling the purpose for which God raised him up in the first place.

## A man for the moment

To understand that purpose and Samson's role in achieving it, we have to see his life and character against the dark background of the age of the Judges. Because of Israel's disobedience and backsliding into idolatry God allowed the nation to suffer humiliation and oppression for forty years under the Philistines. 'Again the Israelites did evil in the eyes of the LORD, so the LORD delivered them into the hands of the Philistines for forty years' (Judges 13:1). Historically this is a picture of a small nation in subjugation to a much stronger power. But spiritually it shows us how God works through historical events to accomplish the ends he desires. The Philistines were to be the means by which he would judge and discipline his people and bring them back to himself, and Samson was to be the man who would begin that process but would not see it through to completion. It is quite wrong to assert, as some writers do, that Samson failed to fulfil God's purpose for him because he did not finally break the domination of the Philistine power over Israel. This in fact did not happen until the reign of king David. But the record is perfectly clear when it says that God chose Samson to '*begin* the deliverance of Israel from the hands of the Philistines' (Judges 13:5).

Samson, as God's man for the moment, was to achieve the limited aim of softening up the Philistines through his mighty exploits, in preparation for the final deliverance of Israel in the time of David. And we are to learn from that the lesson that God, in his wisdom, has specific tasks and objectives for his servants in the ongoing work of his kingdom. Moses began the long trek to the promised land with the Israelites, but he did not enter it. Joshua began the conquest of Canaan, but he did not finish it. David prepared the materials for the building of the temple, but he never saw it built.

Sometimes God calls us to achieve a limited objective. Like Samson, he uses us to begin a process or to set in motion a particular work, but without our ever seeing the final results. If we fail to grasp this lesson it can be painful and discouraging. A pastor may labour faithfully for years in a church and never see the full fruit of blessing in conversions and spiritual growth. But his is a preparatory work which God will then use to bring to fulfilment under his successor in that church. Or we may have been working and praying for a long time for the conversion of a friend or loved one, only to be discouraged by the lack of response. And then suddenly that person comes into contact with another Christian, perhaps away from home, and is gloriously saved. But God would have used our efforts and prayers to begin the process of spiritual awakening in that person's heart. Our Lord's words are so true in this respect, and we should take them to heart: 'the saying "One sows and another reaps' is true. I sent you to reap what you have not worked for. Others have done the hard work, and you have reaped the benefits of their labour' (John 4:37-38).

## Samson's birth and potential

Few men begin life with more favourable promise for the future and with greater potential for God's service than Samson. Like Isaac before him, and John the Baptist and Jesus afterward, the birth of Samson was divinely announced.

> A certain man of Zorah, named Manoah, from the clan of the Danites, had a wife who was sterile and remained childless. The angel of the LORD appeared to her and said, 'You are sterile and childless, but you are going to conceive and have a son' (Judges 13:2-3).

Manoah and his wife were a deeply devout couple who prayed to the Lord (Judges 13:8) for help in rearing the boy who was to be born, and that in itself is a distinct advantage in the upbringing of a child in a godless age such as theirs was, and such as ours is again today. And it is worth noting that Manoah prayed for help before his son was born. Would-be Christian parents would do well to follow his example. Notice too Manoah's question to the angel: 'When your words are fulfilled, what is to be the rule for the boy's life and work?' (Judges 13:12). It was not their intention as parents to bring up Samson in a way that would please only themselves and fulfil their own expectations for him, for they wanted to see God's rule in his life. That must surely say something to all Christian parents today. Ask God to help you bring up your child in a way that pleases him and not only yourself. Give your child clear, spiritual rules and guidance to live by, because in our kind of society no one else is likely to do so.

Samson had a lot going for him right from the start; even his name, which means 'sunny' or 'sunshine', points to the significant role he would play in the history of God's people. As leader and judge he would be like a ray of sunshine in the darkness and discouragement of the times, bringing deliverance to the Israelites from the oppression of the Philistines.

## The Nazirite vow

When Manoah asked the angel by what rule Samson's life was to be governed, the answer was very specific. The angel repeated what he had earlier told Manoah's wife, that the child was to be nurtured according to the Nazirite rule or vow. 'No razor may be used on his head, because the boy is to be a Nazirite, set apart to God from birth . . .' (Judges 13:5). There were other elements in the rule or vow which applied to Manoah's wife, and which she was to observe from the time of Samson's conception in the womb. 'Now see to it that you drink no wine or other fermented drink and that you do not eat anything unclean, because you will conceive and give birth to a son' (Judges 13:4).

This instruction to Manoah's wife shows us what a truly remarkable book the Bible is, and how it anticipates many of the things we like to think are the result of our modern sophisticated approach to life. Today medical science places a great deal of emphasis upon ante-natal care and the importance of expectant mothers refraining from alcohol and tobacco and other substances which can have a harmful effect upon the unborn child. And there are other laws of hygiene in the Bible which anticipate in this way some of the medical problems confronting us today and which, if followed, would make us a happier and healthier people.

The Nazirite vow by which Samson would rule his life is more fully explained in the book of Numbers.

> The LORD said to Moses . . . 'If a man or woman wants to make . . . . a vow of separation to the LORD as a Nazirite, he must abstain from wine and other fermented drink . . . no razor may be used on his head. He must be holy until the period of his separation to the LORD is over . . . he must not go near a dead body. Even if his own father or mother or brother or sister dies, he must not make himself ceremonially unclean . . . Throughout the period of his separation he is consecrated to the LORD' (Numbers 6:1-8).

So what was the significance of the vow for Samson? Taken as a whole it was a vow of separation to God, and it reflected God's intention for Israel as a nation. They were God's covenant people who were meant to live a life separated and different from the culture and idolatry of the surrounding pagan nations. But Israel failed to do so, and now God was raising up a leader in Samson who would live such a separated life and be an example to the nation. But, as we shall see, Samson failed dismally to live up to his Nazirite vow, and in this respect he is a grave warning to us. For believers in Christ are also called to a life of separation, not in the sense of shutting oneself off from normal social life, but in the sense of resisting the allure of the world around us and the temptation to become assimilated into its ways and values. There are three aspects of the Nazirite vow that bear this out.

First, Samson was to abstain from wine and strong drink. We understand this as symbolising a separation from those enjoyments and pleasures which may be legitimate enough in themselves, but for the man pledged to God's service and a leader of God's people they are denied. In short, it is an exercise in personal discipline. When an athlete is in strict training, there will be certain pleasures which he would normally enjoy, but during training he will abstain from them. It is all part of the discipline of separation to get himself in shape for the big event. In the same way the believer will, at certain times perhaps, separate himself from the world and deny himself certain enjoyments as a spiritual discipline, and to get his soul into better shape before God. But, apart from that, all Christians need to keep a careful watch and a tight rein on their pleasures and enjoyments, if they are to serve God at the highest level.

Second, Samson was to abstain from cutting his hair. This symbolised his separation from the normal life and activity of the world to that higher consecrated life centred in God. It was, if you like, a sign or badge which distinguished him from the rest of society and marked him out as God's man and therefore different. So it is with the Christian. There are meant to be certain features about our lifestyle and values which set us apart from others and make us different. Sometimes Christians find this difficult, because there is something in human nature which doesn't like to be different and thus drives us to conform to the world around. But we *are* different simply because God's power through the indwelling Holy Spirit has regenerated and changed us. In Christ we have become 'a new creation; the old has gone, the new has come!' (2 Corinthians 5:17).

Third, Samson was to abstain from any contact with a dead body, human or animal. This symbolised his holiness as God's servant, because contact with the corruption of a corpse made one ceremonially unclean. As Christians we have no need of such ritual cleansing, but the underlying principle still applies. We need to be inwardly holy and clean as God's people. Our churchgoing and outward moral standards may lead the secular world to think of us as clean and holy, and that is not a bad thing since holiness of life will show itself in outward behaviour. But what of our hearts? True holiness comes from within. The interior life is what matters to God in the first instance. It seems that here was Samson's chief weakness. Outwardly through his great feats of strength he helped to deliver Israel from the enemy, but he was never truly delivered on the inside from his own carnal nature. Through his Nazirite vow he was separated to God outwardly, but not inwardly. Even when the Spirit of God came upon him and affected his behaviour so that he was able to accomplish phenomenal feats of strength, his essential character seems to have remained unchanged.

Sanctification or inward cleansing is a work of the Holy Spirit, and we need to give time to it because it doesn't happen overnight. As the hymn rightly says:

> Take time to be holy, the world rushes on;
> Spend much time in secret with Jesus alone.
> By looking to Jesus like Him thou shalt be;
> Thy friends, in thy conduct, His likeness shall see.
> William Dunn Longstaff, 1822-94

## The Spirit's stirring

Following the birth of Samson, it quickly became evident to Manoah and his wife that theirs was no ordinary child. 'The woman gave birth to a boy and named him Samson. He grew and the LORD blessed him, and the Spirit of the LORD began to stir him . . .' (Judges 13:24-25). We are strongly reminded of similar descriptions given of the birth and upbringing of other servants of God in the Bible. 'And the boy Samuel continued to grow in stature and in favour with the LORD and with men' (1 Samuel 2:26). Likewise of John the Baptist: 'And the child grew and became strong in spirit . . .' (Luke 1:80). Also the Lord Jesus: 'And the child grew and became strong; he was filled with wisdom, and the grace of God was upon him' (Luke 2:40).

This similarity with men like Samuel, John the Baptist, and even our Lord, shows the high place Samson had in the purpose of God. But it also shows how far short he fell from that state of grace as he grew to manhood. We are told that as he grew to manhood 'the LORD blessed him'. In what way he was particularly blessed we don't know, but it is enough to know that God's hand was upon him in a special way. This bears out the biblical principle that God has special men for special tasks. Samson was one of them, as was Jeremiah of whom we are told, 'Before I formed you in the womb I knew you, before you were born I set you apart; I appointed you as a prophet to the nations' (Jeremiah 1:5). It was true also of Paul: 'But . . . God, who set me apart from birth and called me by his grace, was pleased to reveal his Son in me so that I might preach him among the Gentiles' (Galatians 1:15-16). To know that God's hand of blessing is on you for some special work or calling is a wonderful thing and a great privilege, and if we are to prove equal to it we must be careful to keep it in the forefront of our minds. It appears that Samson, unlike Samuel and John the Baptist, forgot that early blessing, and as he grew older in years he also grew colder in his spirit.

And yet the other thing we are told about his early upbringing is that 'The Spirit of the LORD began to stir him . . .' (Judges 13:25). Even as a young lad he experienced from time to time some strange intuitive stirring within his own spirit that God had some great work in store for him in the future. At that stage, being young and inexperienced, he may not have fully realised what was happening to him, but the tragedy was that as he grew to maturity he still didn't fully grasp it, so that a day came when the Spirit of God left him and no longer stirred in his soul (Judges 16:20).

What should we learn from that? This surely—that God is not to be trifled with. When by his Spirit God graciously moves within our hearts stirring, prompting, and urging us in a direction in line with his will, we ought not to ignore it or dismiss it as being 'all in the mind'. We ought, at the very least, to pray about it, search the Scriptures seeking further guidance, and talk it over with a trusted Christian friend. God will make such promptings and stirrings clear if we take them seriously. Otherwise we may find, like Samson, that the Spirit of God may never again stir us to undertake some special work, and what a pity that would be!

# 15
# Samson
## and the Spirit of the Lord

*Read Judges 14 and 15*

In these chapters we have the substance of Samson's twenty years as leader and judge in Israel. Whilst they do not make the most edifying reading, they nevertheless reveal how God by his sovereign power can overrule our sins and weaknesses and even use them to further his purposes.

## Samson's sensuality

Not many years had passed before Samson, when still quite young, began to show signs of that headstrong, tempestuous and ill-disciplined nature which was eventually to bring about his downfall.

> Samson went down to Timnah and saw there a young Philistine woman. When he returned, he said to his father and mother, 'I have seen a Philistine woman in Timnah; now get her for me as my wife.' His father and mother replied, 'Isn't there an acceptable woman among your relatives or among all our people? Must you go to the uncircumcised Philistines to get a wife?' (Judges 14:1-3).

The word 'uncircumcised' is used as a term of reproach, meaning that the Philistines were not part of the covenant

people of God, and the Israelites had been expressly com-
manded by God not to intermarry with the pagan nations. In
Samson's case it was doubly sinful, since he was under the
Nazirite vow of separation.

But he was so dominated by self-will and driven by his
passionate nature that he insisted on having his way in spite
of his parents' protests. It was the beginning of that whole
cycle of sinning in his life which shows him as a man driven
by strong sensual feelings, especially where women were
concerned. Indeed he had a fatal weakness in that direction.
In the brief account of his life three emotional entanglements
with women are mentioned, which in all probability repre-
sent many others in the course of his leadership in Israel. The
first was his infatuation with the Philistine woman of Tim-
nah quoted above, and which ended in a short tragic marriage followed by her violent death (Judges 15:1-6). The
second was his association with a Philistine prostitute at
Gaza which almost led to his capture by the enemy (Judges
16:1-3). The third and most tragic of all his entanglements
was his passion for the Philistine Delilah, which ended ultimately in his own death (vv.4-20). We notice also that all
three women came from among pagan Philistines.

Samson's is the old story, so often repeated in history, of a
man strong in other directions of his life and character, but
pitiably weak when it comes to handling his own sexuality.
Samson was hopelessly outflanked by the women in his life,
and when in association with them seems to have been
almost incapable of making any rational judgment. This was
because he was dominated by unrestrained lust and passion.
He is aptly described by Gerald Griffiths as 'the man who
mismanaged his passions'. This failure to control the passions is fatal in a spiritual leader and invariably brings about
his downfall, because it is one of those weaknesses Satan is

quick to exploit in the eyes of the world. Moreover, when a spiritual leader is guilty of a sexual misdemeanour it does incalculable harm to the Church of God and the reputation of the gospel. There is nothing the popular media likes better than a sexual scandal involving Christian leaders, as the many instances we have had in recent years clearly testify.

Our society is obsessed with sex to such a degree that it permeates every aspect of our culture. It is destroying sex as the wonderful pleasurable experience God intended it to be within Christian marriage. Quite apart from the explicitness of sexual material that floods the market through magazines, films, videos, etc., many TV commercials are now full of sensual imagery and innuendo, because manufacturers know that by keeping our sex instincts aflame our sales resistance is lowered as consumers. The whole exercise is a blatant exploitation, of the worst kind, of one of the most precious gifts God has given to mankind, and it shows the murky depths to which we have fallen as a society. The apostle Paul in a powerful passage warns all believers of the dangers of playing fast and loose with sexual feelings.

> Flee from sexual immorality. All other sins a man commits are outside his body, but he who sins sexually sins against his own body. Do you not know that your body is a temple of the Holy Spirit, who is in you, whom you have received from God? You are not your own; you were bought at a price. Therefore honour God with your body (1 Corinthians 6:18-20).

## The Spirit of the Lord

In the light of all that we have said about Samson's lifestyle, it is deeply perplexing to many that three times in his story we are told explicitly that 'The Spirit of the LORD came upon him in power' (Judges 14:6,19; 15:14). In the first place, we have to understand this charismatic anointing within the context of the Old Testament, and not confuse it with the experience of the indwelling of the Holy Spirit for holiness of life taught in the New Testament. In Samson's case the coming of the Spirit's power was always sudden and temporary, to enable him to achieve his mighty exploits in fulfilling God's purpose. In short, the popular notion of Samson as a strong man physically with enormous biceps is totally without foundation. He probably looked no different from the average man in physique. His strength was supernaturally imparted to him in special times of crisis.

In the first instance it enabled him to kill the lion with his bare hands (Judges 14:6); the second was when he slaughtered thirty Philistines at Ashkelon (v.19); the third, when he snapped the ropes that bound him and massacred the Philistines at Lehi (Judges 15:14); and, finally, when he prayed for one more anointing of the Spirit's power to bring down the temple of Dagon on himself and his enemies (Judges 16:28).

There are some important lessons to be learned from this record of the Spirit's activity. First of all, it shows us the sovereign working of the Holy Spirit. The phrase, 'The Spirit of the LORD came upon him in power', is a very distinctive one, since it portrays Samson as the passive recipient, and the Holy Spirit as the active agent, of God's power. In his conversation with Nicodemus the Lord Jesus used a most telling illustration to make this very point: 'The wind blows wherever it pleases. You hear its sound, but you cannot tell where it comes from or where it is going. So it is with everyone born of the Spirit' (John 3:8). We cannot control or direct the activity of the Holy Spirit any more than we can determine the direction of the wind. He is sovereign and free in the way he works; today he convicts a single person here and there to bring him or her to salvation, tomorrow in another part of the world he may come upon hundreds in convicting and converting power. That is his royal prerogative. We can open our lives to his power and pray for it to come upon us and our church in the way his strength came upon Samson, but we cannot manipulate it. One of the saddest features of the 'charismatic' movement in today's Church has been just that —the attempt to manipulate or direct the activity of the Holy Spirit almost to order, so to speak.

Another thing we learn from Samson's experience is that when the Holy Spirit is present in power the evidence is plain enough. He could never have torn the lion apart on his own, or triumphed single-handedly over a thousand Philistines, or carried the gates of Gaza to the top of the hill. These were phenomenal feats of strength, and those who saw them take place would have known that something supernatural was happening. The same is true in times of revival, when the Holy Spirit comes in sudden dramatic outpourings of power. Things happen then which are not the norm in church life. Prayer takes on new meaning and sometimes, as in the 1904–5 Revival in Wales, people lose track of time and prayer meetings go on all through the night. The preaching of the Word is attended with amazing results, hundreds being converted or brought back to renewed commitment to Christ. These and other happenings are the supernatural evidences that the Holy Spirit is present in power.

But we must not run away with the idea that the evidence of the Spirit's power is to be seen only in the dramatic, extraordinary phenomena of revival. When the Lord Jesus illustrated the Spirit's activity in terms of the wind he said to Nicodemus: 'You hear its sound, but you cannot tell where it comes from . . .' We see the evidence of the wind's power not only in the dramatic effects of the hurricane, but also in the gentle rustling of the trees. Likewise we are to know the Spirit's power working in us in a gentle, non-dramatic but equally real way, sanctifying us inwardly in our character. That was Samson's chief weakness. He had the outward dramatic evidences of the Spirit's power, but we do not see that same power at work in his inner life and character.

## Resentment always escalates

Before we leave this part of the story we cannot help noticing how much anger and violence are woven into Samson's life. Chapter fifteen opens with him visiting his wife but being refused permission by her father to see her: 'Samson took a young goat and went to visit his wife. He said, "I'm going to my wife's room." But her father would not let him go in' (Judges 15:1). Insult is added to injury when the father then informs him that his wife has been given in marriage to the best man at his wedding. Samson retaliates by burning the crops of the Philistines, and the Philistines react by burning Samson's wife and father to death. Samson again retaliates by slaughtering a thousand of the Philistines. And so the cycle of resentment and bloodshed continues until eventually both Samson and his enemies perish under the ruins of the temple of Dagon, the Philistine god (Judges 16:23-30).

We realise, of course, that God was using Samson as his instrument to bring about the nation's deliverance from the Philistine enemy, but that is no argument for imitating his violent behaviour. These things are written in Scripture, says Paul, 'as warnings for us, on whom the fulfilment of the ages has come' (1 Corinthians 10:11). So what is the warning? Well, it is telling us that unless we learn, with God's help, to handle the emotion of anger properly, it can have devastating effects and bring about the disintegration of human life. James puts is very powerfully: 'What causes fights and quarrels among you? Don't they come from your desires that battle within you? You want something but don't get it. You kill and covet . . . You quarrel and fight . . .' (James 4:1,2). Uncontrolled resentment always escalates, as in the Samson story.

Today we hear much about what is called 'road rage'. Drivers vent their anger on other motorists, and this often leads to serious acts of violence and even murder. Anger itself is not evil but is a God-given emotion. When the Lord Jesus whipped the money-changers out of the temple for desecrating God's house (John 2:13-17), he was demonstrating a right kind of anger. Likewise, when he got angry with the church leaders who resisted his healing a man on the Sabbath day (Mark 3:5), he was again expressing a righteous form of indignation. We need that right kind of anger: anger that shows itself in opposition to injustice and hypocrisy, to the pornographer and drug-dealer, the drunken motorist, and even church leaders who fail to preach the gospel of salvation in the Lord Jesus Christ. Anger directed, governed, disciplined by the Spirit of God is positive and helpful in bringing an end to the evils in society and creating a happier environment for everyone.

The apostle Paul was absolutely right when he said: 'In your anger do not sin' (Ephesians 4:26). What angers God is not our anger but the abuse of such an emotion, which leads us into sin, and for which we shall be accountable on the Judgment Day.

# 16
# Samson and Delilah

*Read Judges 16*

In this chapter we come to the final tragic days of Samson's life. The story of his relationship with Delilah and the manner in which she betrayed his love, leading to his death at the hands of the Philistines, has become part of the romantic history of the world. Hollywood has exploited the sexual angle for all it is worth; whereas Milton, in his epic poem *Samson Agonistes,* sees the spiritual aspect, recognising with true poetic insight that Samson was as much a betrayer of his Nazirite vow and of God as he was the victim of betrayal by Delilah.

> Nothing of all these evils hath befallen me
> But justly; I myself have brought them on;
> Sole author I, sole cause. If aught seem vile,
> As vile hath been my folly, who have profaned
> The mystery of God, given me under pledge
> Of vow, and have betrayed it to a woman,
> A Canaanite, my faithless enemy.

## Delilah the seductive

It is evident that Samson was hopelessly infatuated with Delilah and was like putty in her hands. She, on the other hand, was quick to exploit his weakness with her seductive charms in order to discover the secret of his great strength.

The rulers of the Philistines went to her and said, 'See if you can lure him into showing you the secret of his great strength and how we can overpower him so that we may tie him up and subdue him. Each one of us will give you eleven hundred shekels of silver' (Judges 16:5).

What followed was treated as a game by Samson. That may have been his biggest mistake because Delilah was deadly serious, and you can't expect to play with fire and not get burned. Three times she tried to get him to reveal his secret. First, he told her to bind him with seven fresh leather thongs and he would become as weak as other men; but he snapped the thongs as easily as 'a piece of string' (Judges 16:6-9). Second, he told her to tie him with new ropes which had never been used; but this too failed at the crucial moment, when he snapped the ropes like threads (Judges 16:10-12). Third, he urged her to weave the seven braids of his hair into the material on the loom; but the moment she called upon the Philistines to overpower him he exerted his enormous strength, pulling away the loom and the shuttle which fastened his hair (Judges 16:13-14). By now the wearing-down process was beginning to take effect:

With such nagging she prodded him day after day until he was tired to death. So he told her everything. 'No razor has ever been used on my head,' he said, 'because I have been a Nazirite set apart to God since birth. If my head were shaved, my strength would leave me, and I would become as weak as any other man' (Judges 16:16-17).

So the secret was out! He had betrayed both his vow and his God.

Having put him to sleep on her lap, she called a man to shave off . . . his hair, and so began to subdue him. And his strength left him. Then she called, 'Samson, the Philistines are upon you!' He awoke from his sleep and thought, 'I'll go out as before and shake myself free.' But he did not know that the LORD had left him (Judges 16:19-20).

What sad words those are! Sadder still, he didn't know that God's power had left him until the moment of crisis came to confront the enemy, and then it was too late. There is no doubt that the believer can lose the power of God's presence in his life without being aware of it, because it can be a slow process happening over a period of time. It can begin with little things, with God gradually being pushed from the centre of one's life to the perimeter as other things crowd in. What starts as an occasional lapse in attending worship becomes, under pressure of work, a regular habit; prayer and the reading of God's Word drop away and fellowship with Christian friends becomes progressively less, until eventually one is left with only the form of religion and without its power. And it may be that, like Samson, it is only when the crisis comes, in the form of sudden bereavement or some other acute trial, that we realise how far we have wandered from God and we do not have the spiritual resources with which to meet that crisis—the power of the Lord has left us.

## Seduction of the world

There is a spiritual sense in which we all have our Delilahs to contend with in this life. The name Delilah is a problem for Bible commentators, with meanings ranging from 'consuming', 'weakening',' debilitating', to 'delicate' or 'dainty'. But all are agreed that, like the name Judas, it has become infamous because of its association with flattery and falseness and the seductive influences that lead people astray and bring destruction in their train. For there is such a spirit of seduction abroad in the world, making what is evil appear glamorous and exciting, while it leads only to moral and spiritual disintegration. Take the enormous social problems associated with young people in our society arising out of the drug culture. Generally speaking, youngsters get hooked on drugs because they are seduced by the promise of an exciting, stimulating experience; but all too often it ends in tragedy.

The Christian too, if he is not careful, can be enticed and seduced by the false glamour and glittering materialism of the world at the expense of destroying his relationship with God. It is for this reason that John warns us against the worldly spirit.

> Do not love the world . . . If anyone loves the world, the love of the Father is not in him. For everything in the world—the cravings of sinful man, the lust of his eyes and the boasting of what he has and does—comes not from the Father but from the world. The world and its desires pass away, but the man who does the will of God lives for ever (1 John 2:15-17).

Then, again, we may feel inclined to blame Samson for being so stupid as to continue trusting Delilah when, on the first three occasions she tried to get his secret from him, she clearly showed her falseness. But he was so blinded by his passion for her that he just couldn't see it or didn't want to believe it. But in any case, don't we have a tendency to do exactly the same thing? Do we always learn from our mistakes? Haven't we, time and time again, proved the falseness of giving ourselves to worldly values? We have experienced

the spiritual hurt it brings and how the power of sin and
Satan can seduce us away from the love of God in Christ, and
yet we return again and again to the same sins. How can we
be so blind? Samson deliberately put himself in the way of
temptation, and so do we. Peter has some harsh, blunt words
to say about those who have tasted of the good things of
God, only to allow themselves again and again to be enticed
and seduced by the same sins and failings. He applies to
them the proverbs, 'A dog returns to its vomit' and 'A sow
that is washed goes back to her wallowing in the mud' (2
Peter 2:22).

## The impotence of Samson

Delilah by her seductiveness and scheming succeeded in
doing to Samson what the lion and the Philistines had failed
to do—destroy him. Yes, we all have our Delilahs, that spirit
of temptation and faithlessness that would seduce us and
drag us away from God in the way the Philistines dragged
Samson to the prison, leaving him blinded, shackled and
impotent. 'Then the Philistines seized him, gouged out his
eyes and took him down to Gaza. Binding him with bronze
shackles, they set him to grinding in the prison' (Judges
16:21). What a sad sight to see God's man defeated spiritually
and morally and left helpless in the hands of the enemy!
From his high calling as the ruler of God's people he was
degraded to the level of an animal grinding corn in the
prison, an object of scorn and mockery. The Philistines were
intoxicated with a sense of triumph in their victory over the
God of Israel.

> Now the rulers of the Philistines assembled to offer a great
> sacrifice to Dagon their god . . . When the people saw him,

they praised their god, saying, 'Our god has delivered our enemy into our hands, the one who laid waste our land and multiplied our slain' (Judges 16:23-24).

There is a sense in which we can see in Samson's predicament a picture of the visible Church as God's servant in today's world. She too is seemingly shackled and bound by a sense of her own impotence and failure in the face of the enemies of the gospel and has become an object of ridicule and mockery to many. And, like Samson, she has brought it on herself by her failure to remain true to her calling to be a light in the sin and darkness of the world by faithfully proclaiming the gospel of Jesus Christ. Take the average Sunday service on TV and you see what I mean. There is little said about the holiness of God, or the nature of sin as a radical alienation from his truth revealed in the gospel, or the necessity of salvation through personal faith in Christ's reconciling death on the cross. Instead, viewers are given a lot of moral platitudes, which leave them completely unmoved and wondering what the difference is between what the Church is saying and what is being said by the politicians and the social planners.

The sad fact is that the visible Church today has, for many years, so diluted the gospel of the good news of God's salvation that few listen to her any more. The divine spiritual strength has left her, just as it left Samson, and the enemies of Christ are laughing and jeering in triumph. 'While they were in high spirits, they shouted, "Bring out Samson to entertain us." So they called Samson out of the prison, and he performed for them' (Judges 16:25). Imagine that—God's servant performing an act to entertain the world! How strongly reminiscent that is of today's Church in going further and further in accommodating the demands of secular society to entertain it rather than to challenge and disturb it with the message of God's truth. Her one aim now, it would seem, is to be popular with the world, to be accepted by it, and to that end she seems perfectly willing to sacrifice in her message any reference to sin, righteousness and the judgment to come.

All that we have said about the visible Church can be true also of the individual Christian. Many, like Samson, are shackled and ineffective in their Christian faith and discipleship because they have trifled with God and allowed Satan, the enemy of their souls, to triumph over them. But it doesn't have to remain like that. The last word doesn't have to be with Satan and the forces of evil. Satan and the enemies of Christ may be laughing and triumphing now, but the last laugh is always with God (see Psalm 2:4; 37:13). History testifies to that in the death of Christ. It seemed on the face of it that, in the darkness of the cross, evil had won, and the enemies of the gospel were triumphant, and the world laughed. But then came the resurrection with its message of hope and victory, and the last word was with God. It seems to me that the same was true of Samson's life; the last word was with God, and it was a word of hope and restoration.

## Repentance

Students of Scripture differ in their interpretation of Samson's death in the temple of Dagon. Some see it as a triumph of restoration, others as a tragedy.

> Samson said to the servant who held his hand, 'Put me where I can feel the pillars that support the temple . . .' Then Samson prayed to the LORD, 'O Sovereign LORD, remember me. O God, please strengthen me just once

more, and let me with one blow get revenge on the Philistines for my two eyes . . . Let me die with the Philistines!' Then he pushed with all his might, and down came the temple on the rulers and all the people in it. Thus he killed many more when he died than while he lived (Judges 16:26-30).

That undoubtedly is tragedy. One writer describes it as 'an act of self-judgment'. And so it was in a way, and therein lies the hope that Samson realised, whilst in the prison, what a fool he had been to stray from God and betray his Nazirite vow. And he despises himself and acknowledges that his bitter end is the judgment he deserves.

There is one sentence in the description of Samson's time spent in the prison which bears out the contention that he had come to a spirit of repentance which led to his restoration with God. 'But the hair on his head began to grow again after it had been shaved' (Judges 16:22). That is significant, because the growth of his hair symbolised his consecration. It is the writer's way of telling us that in the prison Samson had time to reflect and think and had made his peace with God. There are two lessons here.

First, the marks of Samson's sin and disobedience remained with him to the end of his life in the form of his blindness. The consequences of sin and deliberate disobedience to God's will in the life of the believer can sometimes be quite dreadful and leave their mark upon us to the end of our life. No amount of repentance can remove that. God is always ready to forgive our sin and disobedience, but the consequences remain. That is a matter for serious reflection.

Second, Samson's death, and the way in which he met it, tell us that there is always the hope of restoration and peace with God, however far we may have strayed from him. More than that, in spite of the consequences that may follow from our sin, God is always willing, by his Spirit, to help us put the pieces back together again to make something of our lives, and to contribute in a positive way to the ongoing work of his kingdom in the world.

# 17
# Hannah
## a godly mother

*Read 1 Samuel 1*

In studying the character of any great man or woman who has influenced the world, it helps to know something of the home and family into which they were born. What were the parents like, and what were the values that helped to shape and mould their thinking and character in the early years? This is true of Samuel, who was one of the greatest figures in the history of ancient Israel. He was a prophet and judge, and God's instrument in appointing the first king of Israel in the person of Saul. There is no doubt that Samuel owed a great deal to his mother Hannah and to her wisdom and guidance in the early years of his life.

## A God-fearing home

Hannah and Elkanah her husband both loved God and obeyed his law and commandments. Not only did they acknowledge God in their daily lives, but every year Elkanah, his wives Hannah and Peninnah, and his children by Peninnah would make the long, difficult journey from their home town of Ramathaim to the tabernacle or house of God at Shiloh to offer sacrifice and thanksgiving.

Year after year this man went up from his town to worship and sacrifice to the LORD Almighty at Shiloh . . .

> Whenever the day came for Elkanah to sacrifice, he would
> give portions of the meat to his wife Peninnah and to all
> her sons and daughters. But to Hannah he gave a double
> portion because he loved her . . . (1 Samuel 1:3-4).

Here was a godly home in a godless age. This was a
period in Israel's history when the spiritual life of the nation
was at a low ebb; corruption and immorality had affected
every aspect of life and had even polluted the priesthood. Eli
was the chief priest, and his sons Hophni and Phinehas
served under him in the priesthood. But Eli was old and
going blind, and he had lost control of his sons who were
evil men. 'Eli's sons were wicked men; they had no regard
for the LORD' (1 Samuel 2:12). In such a period of darkness
Hannah and Elkanah kept their spiritual integrity and were
determined that their home would be a place where God
was loved and feared and his holy law obeyed.

We cannot help seeing a parallel in all this with our nation
today. Spiritual life is at a low ebb in our country, the
things of God are treated with contempt and indifference
by a large section of the public, the Lord's Day is no longer
kept and honoured, immorality is rife, the Church is weak
and ineffective, and home and family life is breaking
down. We desperately need more godly parents like Hannah and Elkanah, and homes in which children are brought
up in the knowledge of God. It is clear from Genesis 1:27-
28 that the family was intended by God to be the basic unit
of authority and instruction in society, for the instilling of
those values that would help children both in their understanding of God and in becoming law-abiding citizens. It is
not surprising, therefore, that the breakdown in family life
today should lead to the breakdown of life in many other
directions, with all the attendant problems of crime, drug

abuse, drunkenness, violence and other corrupting influences.

## Hannah's problem

In spite of all that was positive in Hannah's home and marriage, she herself had one big problem—she was childless. She desperately wanted a child, but none was forthcoming: 'the LORD had closed her womb' (1 Samuel 1:6). This was a cause of great sadness and heartache to Hannah, especially since among the ancient Israelites the failure to bear children was considered a great reproach and even a sign of God's displeasure. But, as if that in itself was not enough, she had also to put up with the cruel jibes of Peninnah, Elkanah's second wife, who had several children. 'And because the LORD had closed her womb, her rival kept provoking her in order to irritate her. This went on year after year . . .' (1 Samuel 1:6-7). We don't know the circumstances, but it seems likely that Elkanah first married Hannah, whom he loved deeply (1 Samuel 1:5), and when she bore him no children he then married Peninnah who gave him several sons and daughters.

This dissension in an otherwise godly home carries with it its own lesson. Elkanah, like others before him, was reaping the consequences of his own disobedience to God's command in having more than one wife. Be that as it may, Hannah's longing to have a child and Peninnah's mocking attitude had a profound effect upon her. She shows all the signs of a woman in deep depression. 'Elkanah her husband would say to her, "Hannah, why are you weeping? Why don't you eat? Why are you downhearted? Don't I mean more to you than ten sons?"' (1 Samuel 1:8). Had the whole problem become perhaps something of an obsession with Hannah, so that she couldn't enjoy life any more in spite of having a loving husband? She was off her food, and there is even the suggestion that she may have become a little bitter in her spirit (v.10) so that her life was very miserable indeed (v.11).

I see two things here. First, Hannah was in danger of becoming totally negative about her problem. Elkanah's words to her are deeply touching. It is as if he said: 'Hannah, I know you want a child, and so do I; but can't you accept the position as it is? You still have me, a loving and devoted husband; can't you be content with that?' In short, Hannah was becoming so negative that she was overlooking all the positive things in her life for which she could praise and thank God. We can be like that when we have problems and difficulties to face. We can be so negative about them that we can become depressed, lose sleep, go off our food and spend so much time fretting and worrying that it all becomes an obsession and we can make ourselves really ill. This is surely not right for the Christian, however serious the problem. We must be more positive and remind ourselves that there is a God in heaven who is our heavenly Father and knows all about us, and there are still many things in our lives for which we can praise and thank him.

## Praying it through

There came a point, for whatever reason, when Hannah decided to adopt a much more positive attitude. She took her problem to God in prayer.

> In bitterness of soul Hannah wept much and prayed to the LORD. And she made a vow, saying, 'O LORD Almighty, if you will only look upon your servant's misery and remember me, and not forget your servant but give her a

son, then I will give him to the LORD for all the days of his life . . .' (1 Samuel 1:10).

Today the problem of women not being able to conceive and bear children is the focus of a lot of attention by government departments and the medical authorities, and millions of pounds are spent in attempting to resolve it through the latest technology, but not always successfully.

But what a sad and confused state our nation is in regarding moral and spiritual values when, at the other end of the scale, we have thousands of mothers every year aborting babies for the most trivial reasons. Will we ever get it right with respect to the increasing number of ethical problems facing us as a result of scientific progress? Not, it would seem, until we follow the line of Hannah and bring God into the equation. This does not mean for one moment that prayer is a short-cut answer to childlessness or any other problem that may face us. Let us make use of whatever help is available, scientific or otherwise, but let us also take on board the reminder, from Hannah's approach, that prayer changes our attitude to our particular problem and enables us to handle it more efficiently. That was certainly true for her. Following her prayer she was an entirely different woman. Her depression was gone, her appetite for food returned, and she was spiritually and psychologically much more positive when she and Elkanah left the sanctuary to return home. 'Then she went her way and ate something, and her face was no longer downcast' (1 Samuel 1:18).

She had not received an answer to her prayer as yet, but the very act of praying and taking her problem to God had had a profound effect upon her. She had learned something about herself and her tendency to be negative about things. And that is what prayer does for us if we take it seriously.

We pray about the matter in hand and we then leave it with God. We no longer fret about it and make ourselves ill and depressed with worry, but we accept the situation as it is and believe that God will do whatever is right and best for us, and that gives a peace to our hearts.

## Hannah's sacrifice

In due time Hannah received a positive answer to her prayer. 'So in the course of time Hannah conceived and gave birth to a son. She named him Samuel, saying "Because I asked the LORD for him"' (1 Samuel 1:20). One would have thought that was the end of the matter. Hannah had now received from God what to her would become her most precious possession. But she then did a most remarkable thing. In her prayer she had already vowed that if God would give her a son she would give him back to the Lord to serve him in his sanctuary for the rest of his life. '". . . if you will . . . not forget your servant but give her a son, then I will give him to the LORD for all the days of his life . . ."' (1 Samuel 1:11).

This was a remarkable act of self-sacrifice. She had longed for this child more than anything else in all the world, and now that she had him she was willing to give him back to God. If anything speaks to us of the place God held in the heart and life of Hannah, this must surely be it. And sometimes God asks that of us: as a proof of our love for him and the central place he has in our lives, to give him our most precious possession. This happened with Abraham.

> Some time later God tested Abraham . . . Then God said, 'Take your son, your only son, Isaac, whom you love, and go to the region of Moriah. Sacrifice him there as a burnt offering on one of the mountains I will tell you about' (Genesis 22:1-2).

Just as Hannah had longed for her child Samuel, so Abraham and Sarah had longed for the promised son Isaac. And now here was God asking them to give him up—their most precious possession!

Why should God do this? Was it because Abraham was in danger of loving Isaac more than he loved God? That is what can happen to the things that are precious to us in this life; they can nudge God out of the central place in our affection. That most precious object of our affection can be almost anything: a wife or husband, a job or career, a hobby or friend, our home or family, our ambition or wealth. The point is, these are not bad in themselves; but it shows that what is good can keep us from what is much better where God is concerned, his love and blessing in our lives.

## Hannah kept her vow

Something like three years must have elapsed from the time Hannah made her vow to dedicate her child Samuel to the Lord and the day when she actually put it into practice. The bond between mother and child would have been very strong by this time, and Hannah might have forgotten altogether the vow she had made under the emotional stress of the moment. But that didn't happen. She kept her vow to God.

> After he was weaned, she took the boy with her, young as he was, along with a three-year-old bull . . . to the house of the LORD at Shiloh. When they had slaughtered the bull, they brought the boy to Eli, and she said to him . . . 'I prayed for this child, and the LORD has granted me what I asked of him. So now I give him to the LORD. For his whole life he shall be given over to the LORD.' And he worshipped the LORD there (1 Samuel 1:24-28).

When Hannah made her promise to God to give back her child for his service she really meant it, and she carried out her promise although it must have cost her a great deal in terms of loneliness and heartache. In this beautiful way she anticipated our Lord's words when he said, 'Simply let your "Yes" be "Yes", and your "No", "No"; anything beyond this comes from the evil one' (Matthew 5:37). He meant that we should say what we mean and mean what we say; we should not trivialise the truth in any way. This is what we do when we lightly and thoughtlessly make promises to God and other people and fail to keep them. Promises made at marriage before God are being broken every day by Christians and non-Christians alike, as divorce statistics make abundantly clear.

What we are really talking about here is respect for the truth and the value we put upon the words we speak. We are living in a day of double-talk, when people *say* one thing and *mean* something different, or else the words they speak and the promises made are emptied of value and meaning. It happens all the time. You take your car into the local garage and you are told that it will be ready the following morning. But even as the words are spoken you know the car will not be ready for at least a couple of days. The phrase 'credibility gap' is now common parlance for the difference between what a politician says on TV for public consumption, and what we know he really means beneath the surface. All this shows an utter contempt for the truth, and for the value of words as a reflection of our hearts, and is severely condemned by the Lord Jesus Christ. 'But I tell you that men will have to give an account on the day of judgment for every careless word they have spoken. For by your words you will be acquitted, and by your words you will be condemned' (Matthew 12:36-37).

We ought not to make promises to God or to other people thoughtlessly and lightly, especially if we know at the time that there is little chance of our keeping them. And when we make a promise, let us, like Hannah, mean it and keep to it. We read in Scripture, 'For no matter how many promises God has made, they are "Yes" in Christ' (2 Corinthians 1:20). God keeps his promises to us, and we expect him to do so. Why shouldn't he expect us in Christ to do the same?

# 18
# Nabal and Abigail
## an ill-suited couple

*Read 1 Samuel 25*

We may wonder sometimes why certain couples ever married each other, for they seem so ill-suited in character and temperament. More than once, I have heard someone say in absolute amazement, 'I don't know what she sees in him/her.' But that's just it. He or she sees in the other something the rest of us do not see, and in spite of their obvious differences in character and outlook, or perhaps because of them, their marriage is a roaring success. The same, sadly, could be said of Nabal and Abigail, who are the subjects of this chapter. She was as beautiful and intelligent and God-fearing as he was surly, foolish and God-denying.

A certain man in Maon, who had property there at Carmel, was very wealthy. He had a thousand goats and three thousand sheep, which he was shearing in Carmel. His name was Nabal and his wife's name was Abigail. She was an intelligent and beautiful woman, but her husband, a Calebite, was surly and mean in his dealings' (1 Samuel 25:2-3).

The background to the story is this: David and his men were on the run from Saul in the desert of Maon, where he received material support from the local landowners of Judah in return for protecting their shepherds and flocks from bands of Philistine raiders. On this particular occasion, David sent his men to Nabal for food and hospitality in return for his services. It was sheep-shearing time and a festive season (v.8), when generosity and giving were the order of the day. But the men received only contempt and insults.

> Nabal answered David's servants, 'Who is this David? Who is this son of Jesse? Many servants are breaking away from their masters these days. Why should I take my bread and water, and the meat I have slaughtered for my shearers, and give it to men coming from who knows where?' (vv.10-11).

This was a pretty ugly response, since David was not begging but seeking fair payment for services rendered. One of Nabal's own servants confirmed this when he reported the matter to his master's wife Abigail.

> David sent messengers from the desert to give our master his greetings, but he hurled insults at them. Yet these men are very good to us. They did not ill-treat us, and the whole time we were out in the fields near them nothing was missing. Night and day they were a wall around us all the time we were herding our sheep near them. Now think it over and see what you can do, because disaster is hanging over our master and his whole household. He is such a wicked man that no-one can talk to him (vv.14-16).

## His ingratitude

Nabal was a man whose nature matched his name, which means 'fool'. That was also his wife's estimate of him when she later spoke to David: 'May my lord pay no attention to that wicked man Nabal. He is just like his name—his name is Fool, and folly goes with him' (v.25). She may have been trying in this way to excuse her husband's churlish behaviour and ingratitude by attributing it to natural weakness and lack of understanding. But can ingratitude and thanklessness ever be excused? Give him a bone, and even a dog will wag his tail!

The truth is that ingratitude is among the most common of sins and we can all be guilty of it at some time or other. There are few of us who have not at some time been greatly indebted for a kindness shown to us. But have we always been grateful and taken the trouble to express our thankfulness and appreciation? Children, even as adults, can be very ungrateful to parents, especially when they are old and feeble and are in need of love and support. Paul, in his second letter to Timothy, sees ingratitude on the part of children to parents as a characteristic of the decadence in the last days. 'But mark this: There will be terrible times in the last days. People will be lovers of themselves, lovers of money, boastful, proud, abusive, disobedient to their parents, ungrateful . . .' (2 Timothy 3:1-2). Shakespeare's King Lear says: 'How sharper than a serpent's tooth it is / To have a thankless child.'

But most hurtful of all is our ingratitude in relation to God's mercies. Remember how our Lord Jesus referred to this in the healing of the ten lepers? Only one returned to give thanks and drew from our Lord the comment: 'Were not all ten cleansed? Where are the other nine? Was no-one found to return and give praise to God except this foreigner?' (Luke 17:17). The Psalmist said: 'Praise the LORD, O my soul, and forget not all his benefits' (Psalm 103:2). But that is exactly what we are guilty of so often—we forget to praise God for his blessings. We praise him when we have something special to praise him for, and we do it with great meaningfulness and intensity; but then time passes and we forget to thank him for all the daily benefits we enjoy. But God doesn't want us to remember his goodness only when something special happens in our lives, or when it is wrung out of us by the desperation of our circumstances. He wants our gratitude and praise to arise spontaneously out of the depths of our hearts on a daily basis for all the benefits he lavishes upon us.

## No place for God

From what we are told about Nabal it seems he gave no place to God in his life. He was very wealthy and 'surly and mean in his dealings' and both his wife and his servant describe him as a wicked man (1 Samuel 25:17,25). It seems his wealth had gone to his head and made him arrogant and proud, with no time for God or man because of his unteachable spirit. The complaint of his servant was that 'no-one can talk to him'. He was the kind of man you couldn't reason with or seek to help because of his self-sufficiency. He enjoyed the good life his great wealth could give him, so that he lived like a king, and beyond that he felt no sense of need of anyone, not even of God himself.

> When Abigail went to Nabal, he was in the house holding a banquet like that of a king. He was in high spirits and very drunk. So she told him nothing until day-break. Then in the morning, when Nabal was sober, his wife told him all these things, and his heart failed him and he became like a stone. About ten days later, the LORD struck Nabal and he died (vv.36-38).

He probably suffered a stroke brought on by the shock and

fright of hearing how close he had been to death in view of David's threat to take his life.

Nabal reminds us of that other rich fool our Lord spoke of in his parable (Luke 12:13-21). He, too, gave all his time and thought to money and living a life of luxury, with never a thought for God. But both had their life taken from them suddenly and were stripped naked of everything except their immortal souls to appear before God at the judgment. Little wonder our Lord ended his parable by saying, 'This is how it will be with anyone who stores up things for himself but is not rich towards God.' How foolish it is to spend so much time and energy on caring, nourishing, pampering and clothing our bodies, and never spending so much as five minutes caring for our souls! That is not to say that the material possessions and comforts of life are not to be enjoyed. They too are God-given and he wants us to enjoy them. But when the Lord Jesus said, 'Do not store up for yourselves treasures on earth' (Matthew 6:19), he was telling us to adopt a certain attitude to material things. The expression 'store up' means we shouldn't become obsessed with them, or let them get such a grip on us so that they claim all our time and attention, with the result that no room is left for God in our lives.

## Abigail's character

When we turn to Nabal's wife, we are dealing with an altogether different kind of person. She possessed all those finer qualities of character that her husband lacked. She was a beautiful and intelligent woman, with a gracious manner and a deep faith in God. Her tact and wisdom are to be seen in the way she acted in the crisis facing her husband's household because of his contemptuous reply to David. When

David's men reported to him what Nabal had said he went berserk. His response was totally irrational and he lost all self-control.

> David said to his men, 'Put on your swords!' . . . and David put on his. About four hundred men went up with David . . . David had just said, 'It's been useless—all my watching over this fellow's property in the desert so that nothing of his was missing . . . May God deal with David, be it ever so severely, if by morning I leave alive one male of all who belong to him!' (vv.13,21-22).

If Abigail had not intervened to calm David's violent reaction, the result would have been disastrous, but she was a true peacemaker. She sized up the situation in a moment and acted swiftly by taking a peace offering to David in the form of supplies to his men.

> Abigail lost no time. She took two hundred loaves of bread, two skins of wine, five dressed sheep, five seahs of roasted grain, a hundred cakes of raisins and two hundred cakes of pressed figs, and loaded them on donkeys. Then she told her servants, 'Go on ahead; I'll follow you.' But she did not tell her husband Nabal (vv.18-19).

What a wise woman she was! But that was not all. David was in great danger of losing all control over his feelings and in a single outburst of anger would have wrecked all the plans God had for him. He had a hard lesson to learn, and God chose to use Abigail to teach it to him.

## The lesson of self-control

If David had followed his original intention, not only would he have committed a great sin in the massacre of Nabal's household, but he would have done his own cause irreparable harm. He would have lost the support of the other great landowners of Judah, for obviously, if he couldn't control his own feelings, what hope was there of him ever controlling and governing the nation?

In our society today 'self-control' is almost a dirty word. And yet in the New Testament it is listed among the fruit of the Spirit (Galatians 5:22). It is difficult in our kind of society to live a life of self-control and discipline, since there is so much that militates against it. Ours is supposedly the age of liberation and freedom, in which people are meant to find fulfilment of their true selves. The 'free expressionists' in education, the 'women's lib movement', and the 'progressives' in politics and on the social scene have all had their say for a long time now, and any suggestion of the need for self-control and discipline as an essential ingredient in society has been howled down as an interference in the freedom of the individual.

But what has been the effect of all this talk about freedom and self-expression? It is leading to the steady disintegration of society. In the above passage in Galatians, Paul makes the point that uncontrolled freedom always leads to licence and destruction.

> You, my brothers, were called to be free. But do not use your freedom to indulge the sinful nature . . . If you keep on biting and devouring each other, watch out or you will be destroyed by each other (Galatians 5:13,15).

That is precisely what is happening today. Society is being destroyed and devoured by the excesses of uncontrolled emotions, appetites and fleshly indulgence. We see it in every walk of life—entertainment, sport, the mass media, and public and political life. It was said of Alexander the Great that he conquered the world, but he never succeeded in conquering himself. All his life he suffered from a lack of self-discipline and control. He defeated the world, and yet he would weep and curse because he was so pathetically defeated by his own passions and excesses.

David was in great danger of destroying his own character in the eyes of the people and of frustrating God's purpose for him to become the king of all Israel. Had it not been for Abigail, who persuaded him not to act in this uncontrolled and vengeful manner, he may well have never become king. She gave him two reasons why he should not take this action.

First, she pointed out that he was God's man destined for kingship and was engaged in the Lord's work and battle. 'Please forgive your servant's offence, for the LORD will certainly make a lasting dynasty for my master, because he fights the LORD's battles. Let no wrongdoing be found in you as long as you live' (1 Samuel 25:28). Like David, believers are God's people and are destined for great things. We, too, are engaged in the work and battle of God's kingdom, but we must realise that Satan carries the warfare into the area of our personal lives and emotions. Every time he succeeds in making us the victim of our own uncontrolled desires and appetites, he wins a real moral and spiritual victory. Whenever there is the temptation for this to happen, therefore, we need to remind ourselves that we belong to God, we have within us the Holy Spirit, and we are called to a sanctified and holy life.

Second, Abigail reminded David that to give way to this act of uncontrolled passion would lead to a loss of personal respect and dignity and would destroy his peace both with God and with himself. 'When the LORD has done for my master every good thing he promised concerning him and has appointed him leader over Israel, my master will not have on his conscience the staggering burden of needless bloodshed or of having avenged himself' (vv.30-31). For some Christians, their greatest problem is living with something they have said or done, for which they can never really forgive themselves, in spite of the fact that they have repented of it and know that God in Christ has forgiven them. That is one of the most dreadful things about sin; it always leaves its mark and we have to live with it. Sometimes something said or done keeps coming back to haunt us and can make our life a misery.

In Genesis, we have the story of Joseph, who had many bad memories of the things he had suffered at the hands of his brothers and other people. But he named his first son Manasseh—'because God has made me forget all my trouble and all my father's household' (Genesis 41:51). The best we can do, if we find it difficult to forgive ourselves for things said or done, is to ask God to take the sting out of the memory when it returns. It seems that David learned the lesson of self-control which God was teaching him through Abigail, and it would pay us to do the same.

David said to Abigail, 'Praise be to the LORD, the God of Israel, who has sent you today to meet me. May you be blessed for your good judgment and for keeping me from bloodshed this day and from avenging myself with my own hands' (1 Samuel 25:32-33).

# 19
# Absalom
### the cunning egotist

*Read 2 Samuel 13–18*

T he words that spring to mind when considering the character of Absalom are these: unscrupulous, greedy, untrustworthy, scheming, ambitious and suchlike. He was an important figure in the history of Israel, and the fact that six chapters are devoted to his story is an indication of that. He was the third son of king David, and a royal prince who undoubtedly would have succeeded his father to the throne had he acted differently from the way he did.

## Outward appearance

Our first impression of Absalom is of a man obsessed with his public image. He certainly was handsome, with a fine princelike appearance and great charm, and when it came to popular opinion in the country he seems to have been a real favourite with many of the people. We get a glimpse of his all-absorbing egotism right at the outset.

> In all Israel there was not a man so highly praised for his handsome appearance as Absalom. From the top of his head to the sole of his foot there was no blemish in him. Whenever he cut the hair of his head—he used to cut his hair from time to time when it became too heavy for

him—he would weigh it, and its weight was two hundred shekels by the royal standard (2 Samuel 14:25-26).

We feel that if only Absalom could have matched on the inside of his character what he was on the outside, he would have made a great king. But he didn't have what it takes to be a great national leader, certainly not in God's sight, for he was too vain and superficial and eaten up with egotism. This view of his character is confirmed by what we are finally told of him:

> During his life-time Absalom had taken a pillar and erected it in the King's Valley as a monument to himself . . . He named the pillar after himself, and it is called Absalom's Monument to this day (2 Samuel 18:18).

Image-making is something we are all too familiar with in our day. So many seem to be engaged in it—pop stars, politicians, sports figures and even famous evangelists are all concerned to portray the right kind of public image. I suppose to a certain degree we are all involved in this since we consider important what others think of us. We want them to have what we think are the right ideas about us. But is there not a danger that we can get too wrapped up in ourselves, almost egocentric and always worrying about the opinions of others? Such an attitude can make life unbearable and, from the Christian standpoint, is a sign of spiritual immaturity.

It means that we are taking the opinions and assessments of others as a guide to the kind of people we should be. Not that what others think of us is unimportant, but of much greater importance is what God thinks of us. Remember what Paul says? 'The spiritual man makes judgments about all things, but he himself is not subject to any man's judgment' (1 Corinthians 2:15). What does he mean? Simply this, that other people's judgments about us are not the last word, for they are sinful like ourselves. We are to live to please God; that is to be our first aim, not to please others. If others don't like what they see in us, then we must not be put out by that. What God thinks of us is what matters in the end.

## An ambitious spirit

Absalom's egotism and self-love also showed itself in the spirit of aggressive and ruthless ambition that drove him to seek the throne of his father David, irrespective of the hurt inflicted on others. He was utterly ruthless in pursuing that objective. Earlier he had murdered his half-brother, in revenge for the rape of his sister Tamar, and because Amnon preceded him in the line of succession to the throne: 'Absalom ordered his men, "Listen! When Amnon is in high spirits from drinking wine and I say to you, 'Strike Amnon down,' then kill him"' (2 Samuel 13:28). For four years (2 Samuel 15:7) he plotted and schemed to overthrow his father David, showing skill and cunning in manipulating the people to support his revolt.

> In the course of time, Absalom provided himself with a chariot and horses and with fifty men to run ahead of him. He would get up early and stand by the side of the road leading to the city gate. Whenever anyone came with a complaint to be placed before the king for a decision, Absalom would call out to him . . . 'If only I were appointed judge in the land! Then everyone who has a complaint or case could come to me and I would see that he receives justice.' Also, whenever anyone approached him to bow

down before him, Absalom would reach out his hand,
take hold of him and kiss him. Absalom behaved in this
way towards all the Israelites who came to the king asking
for justice, and so he stole the hearts of the men of Israel
(2 Samuel 15:1-6).

In the light of the above we can ask the question: Is it
wrong for the Christian to be ambitious and to seek success
in this life? Is it wrong to go after the material prizes of this
world and to make plans for the betterment of ourselves and
our children? The immediate answer is no. After all, plenty
of people in the Bible who received God's approval were
immensely successful in public life: Joseph, Daniel, Nehemiah and David, for example. And Christians like Lydia and
Philemon seem to have been very successful and wealthy.
Nowhere in the Old Testament do we find teaching that is
anti-material or that encourages a harsh, demanding existence in this life.

But there are plenty of warnings about the dangers of an
ambitious spirit and the all-absorbing pursuit of the glittering prizes of this world. Ambition is associated with 'potential', and God wants us to fulfil our potential as human
beings. But ambition becomes wrong and destructive when
it takes over and God is left out of the equation. Our ambition becomes misdirected when its sole object is to satisfy our
own desires and provide us with gratification, rather than to
fulfil God's purpose in our lives. That is where Absalom
went wrong. His relentless ambition to be king took over his
life, so that all scruples were thrown aside and success
became more important than truth, dignity, integrity, honesty and the worship of God.

And if that was true of him in that far-off, primitive age,
how much more real is the danger of it happening to us in a

consumer-driven society, in which we are constantly pressurised to be successful and to drive ourselves like machines in order to obtain the maximum number of the glittering prizes of this life? May God help us to heed Paul's wise advice:

> Do nothing out of selfish ambition or vain conceit, but in humility consider others better than yourselves. Each of you should look not only to your own interests, but also to the interests of others (Philippians 2:3-4).

## The devil's schemes

We have seen in the passage above how Absalom with great cunning followed a definite strategy for four years to seduce the people from their love and loyalty to king David and to win them to his own cause. He would stand at the city gate early in the morning and insinuate that those with grievances were not getting a fair hearing from the king, and that if he were in power things would be very different. Moreover, he presented himself as the people's champion, an 'ordinary sort of bloke' in spite of his princely status, by shaking them by the hand and even kissing them on occasion. And all this was done in such a subtle and insidious manner that the people were not aware of what was happening to their loyalties, and so we read: 'he stole the hearts of the men of Israel' (2 Samuel 15:6).

In all this Absalom was the tool of Satan, and he is a warning to us of how easily and subtly Satan can steal from our hearts our love and loyalty to Christ our King. It is not for nothing that Paul tells believers: 'Put on the full armour of God so that you can take your stand against the devil's schemes' (Ephesians 6:11). In the warfare of the Spirit Satan is a wily tactician who will use every trick in the book to seduce us from our love for the Lord Jesus. It is not always the frontal attack. It can all begin in simple ways: a slight cooling-off when it comes to the reading of God's Word and the 'quiet time'; then a negligence creeps in regarding the worship of a Sunday; and so it goes on, one little thing after another, but all subtly and insidiously drawing away the love of our hearts for the things of God. And if we are not careful it might even lead to open rebellion in the way that the people supported Absalom's cause in his revolt against king David. We will not be the first believers to wake up suddenly one day to experience what William Cowper speaks of in his hymn:

> Where is the blessedness I knew
>   When first I saw the Lord?
> Where is the soul-refreshing view
>   Of Jesus and His Word?

## A shameful end

In the battle which followed his rebellion, all Absalom's dreams of royal power and self-aggrandisement came to an end with his own miserable death, and 'he was buried like a dog in a lonely wood'.

> Now Absalom . . . was riding his mule, and as the mule went under the thick branches of a large oak, Absalom's head got caught in the tree. He was left hanging in mid-air, while the mule he was riding kept on going . . . Joab . . . took three javelins in his hand and plunged them into Absalom's heart while Absalom was still alive in the oak tree . . . They took Absalom, threw him into a big pit in the forest and piled a large heap of rocks over him (2 Samuel 18:9,14,17).

There are two lessons to be drawn from Absalom's miserable end.

(a) First, as he hung in the tree a helpless target, deserted by his men and knowing that his life would be taken from him at any moment, did he think of God? We don't know. It is said that when a man is drowning his whole past life flashes through his mind in a moment. I don't know if that is true, but it may have been true of Absalom in his final moments. It is a dreadful thing to leave this life when you are still the enemy of God, as he was up to that moment. Did he perhaps, for the first time, see with blinding clarity that his grasping ambition, his vanity and pride, his ruthlessness and cunning in using other people for his own profit—all these things had let him down in the end, and there was nothing now in this world that he had striven so hard to possess that could help him at the last to meet with God?

That surely is a warning to us that we cannot leave it to the final moments of life to put things right with our Maker. We dare not think that there is plenty of time to deal with such serious matters, and that life right now is for living and enjoyment. The truth is that the only time we have is *now*, and it is now that we need to get right with God. Otherwise, as the Bible says, 'It is a dreadful thing to fall into the hands of the living God' (Hebrews 10:31).

(b) Absalom's death teaches us that, if we are not careful, what we regard as the chief glory in our life can become the chief cause of our downfall. It was his glorious head of hair in which he took such pride that brought about Absalom's death. There are things in our lives which are not wrong in themselves, but which can become a snare and a hindrance to our spiritual well-being if we do not keep a tight rein on them, and if we allow them to take the place and glory that

Clearly she took the matter of providing food and shelter for the prophet very seriously, and regarded it as a real ministry for God. At first it was the occasional meal, but then she went further and suggested to her husband that they build an extension to the home solely for the prophet's use. She evidently was in a position to do this since she is described as a 'well-to-do' woman. But what a gracious act! Some years ago I was on holiday in Cornwall with my family and we visited an old stonemason's cottage in Trewent. The original owner had built on to it a little room, just like that mentioned in our passage, containing a table, bed, lamp and chair for the use of John Wesley during his itinerant ministry in that part of the country. I recall being deeply moved as I stood with my family in that simple room and prayed, because I felt it had been sanctified by the godly presence of Wesley more than if I had been standing in St Paul's Cathedral.

In the New Testament Church, itinerant preachers like Paul and John valued highly the hospitality and practical support given them by God's people. Paul in his letter to Philemon actually asks him to prepare the guest room in readiness for his next visit. 'And one thing more: Prepare a guest room for me, because I hope to be restored to you in answer to your prayers' (Philemon 22). John praised Gaius for opening his home to the travelling preachers in the Church.

> Dear friend, you are faithful in what you are doing for the brothers, even though they are strangers to you. They have told the church about your love. You will do well to send them on their way in a manner worthy of God. It was for the sake of the Name that they went out, receiving no help from the pagans. We ought therefore to show hospitality to such men so that we may work together for the truth (3 John 5-8).

It was through the hospitality she gave to Paul and his friends that the Philippian church had its beginnings in the home of Lydia (Acts 16:15,40). Priscilla and Aquila are a couple frequently mentioned in Acts whose home was greatly used in the service of God. Paul made it the base for his operations in Corinth (Acts 18:1-3). Apollos received their hospitality in Ephesus (Acts 18:26), and on two occasions mention is made of 'the church that meets at their house' (Romans 16:5 and 1 Corinthians 16:19).

From these and many other passages in the New Testament it is evident that what the Shunammite woman did for Elisha in providing hospitality was something greatly approved of by God, and a ministry all believers should take very seriously. Our homes can be strategic centres for God to use—in providing hospitality for visiting preachers and missionaries to our local church, as a base for house-groups and the conduct of meetings, as places for witness by inviting friends and neighbours in to listen to a Christian tape or watch a Christian video. Indeed we should be so thankful to God that we have our comfortable homes that using them in his service becomes almost an obligation. There are thousands of people in our towns and cities who have no real home, not to mention the millions throughout the world living in refugee camps without either home or country. Is it too much therefore that we, who have the material means, like the woman of Shunem, should see our homes as one way of expressing our love for the gospel by using them in God's service in whatever ways we can?

It is surely not without some significance that among the last of our Lord's earthly concerns when on the cross was the well-being of his mother whom he committed to the care of his disciple John, of whom we read, 'from that time on, this disciple took her into his own home' (John 19:27).

## She was content

Elisha was mindful of all the trouble the Shunammite had gone to on his behalf and he showed his appreciation by asking her if he could use his influence as a man of God to help her in any way.

> One day when Elisha came, he went up to his room and lay down there. He said to his servant Gehazi, 'Call the Shunammite.' So he called her, and she stood before him. Elisha said to him, 'Tell her, "You have gone to all this trouble for us. Now what can be done for you? Can we speak on your behalf to the king or the commander of the army?"' She replied, 'I have a home among my own people' (2 Kings 4:11-13).

Her reply makes it clear that she was perfectly content with her lot in life; there was nothing she craved for or envied in others that could in any considerable degree add to her happiness and sense of well-being. She had her home, she had friends among her own people and she worshipped the true God of Israel—with that she was wholly satisfied. To have such a spirit of contentment in life is a great blessing, and the distinct lack of it, perhaps more than anything else, is what characterises the life of our modern society. There is at the heart of our nation an ugly itching covetousness and greed that creates a restlessness in people as they eagerly grasp for more and more things. In commercial and public life it is evidenced by such popular phrases as 'the unacceptable face of capitalism', 'the politics of envy' and 'the politics of greed'. Added to the other forms of gambling already in existence, the introduction of the National Lottery with its promise to make one a millionaire overnight has deepened still further this covetous spirit, and made us a nation of gamblers. But, over and above all this, the spirit of discontent and restlessness is most evident in the general disagreeableness of our society and the poor quality of life characterised by rising crime, increased divorce, the breakdown of family life, the growing brutality towards children and the elderly, and the widespread drug culture among young people. Added to this is the growing number of people suffering from stress and nervous disorders, and the increase in suicide in the 18 to 25 age group. These are all symptoms of a discontented and unhappy people who, in the words of the apostle Paul, are 'without hope and without God in the world' (Ephesians 2:12).

There are perhaps a few people born with a quiet contented spirit, but for most of us it is something that has to be cultivated and learned, and that becomes terribly difficult in an acquisitive society like ours in which there are powerful forces deliberately aimed at making us discontented with what we already have. We are bombarded daily through TV commercials and the high pressure techniques of big business to indulge more and more in surrounding ourselves with the glittering toys and trinkets of our consumer society which we neither need nor can afford. But in spite of these outward pressures, the Bible teaches us that the spirit of true contentment in Christ can be cultivated in our lives with all its attendant joys and blessings. The apostle Paul himself is a good example of this. He was not a naturally contented man, but he learned with the help of Christ to become one.

I know what it is to be in need, and I know what it is to have plenty. I have learned the secret of being content in any and every situation . . . I can do everything through him who gives me strength (Philippians 4:12-13).

It is as we submit ourselves more and more to the sanctifying work of the Holy Spirit that we can experience in growing measure what the Puritan writer Jeremiah Burroughs calls *The Rare Jewel of Christian Contentment.*[1] Like a jewel, a spirit of contentment is both rare and precious, but well worth striving after in Christ, and when learned it enriches our lives beyond belief.

## She doubted God's promise

Although the Shunammite woman had said she wanted nothing in return for her kindness, Elisha nevertheless felt there must be something he could do for her as a token of his gratitude. So he mentions it to his servant Gehazi.

> 'What can be done for her?' Elisha asked. Gehazi said, 'Well, she has no son and her husband is old.' Then Elisha said, 'Call her.' So he called her, and she stood in the doorway. 'About this time next year,' Elisha said, 'you will hold a son in your arms.' 'No, my lord,' she objected. 'Don't mislead your servant, O man of God!' (2 Kings 4:14-16).

To have a child, especially a son, was the deepest desire of every Israelite woman, but this was something the Shunammite, with an elderly husband, had not even considered remotely possible in her situation; hence her objection to the prophet making a promise he could not fulfil. But she was overlooking one very important factor. Elisha was not making the promise on his own behalf but on the basis of God's power to fulfil it. And so it turned out. 'But the woman became pregnant, and the next year about that same time she gave birth to a son, just as Elisha had told her' (v.17). That God always keeps his promises is the clear testimony of

1   Banner of Truth, Edinburgh

Scripture. Abraham and Sarah had to learn that lesson the hard way. They too were promised a son by God, and like the Shunammite they too doubted it could happen, because they were old and past the child-bearing age.

> Then the LORD said, 'I will surely return to you about this time next year, and Sarah your wife will have a son' . . . So Sarah laughed to herself as she thought, 'After I am worn out and my master is old, will I now have this pleasure?' Then the LORD said to Abraham, 'Why did Sarah laugh and say, "Will I really have a child, now that I am old?" Is anything too hard for the LORD?' (Genesis 18:10-14).

That is the question we must really face up to in relation to the promises of God—'Is anything too hard for the LORD?' If we can answer that with a resounding 'No', then we can rest on the promises of Scripture and apply them to our own lives. This is the point Paul makes when he says: 'For no matter how many promises God has made, they are "Yes" in Christ. And so through him the "Amen" is spoken to us to the glory of God' (2 Corinthians 1:20). What a tremendous encouragement that is!—for example, to ministers of the gospel who find it such a hard struggle to continue preaching in a godless age like ours when the things of the Spirit are held in such contempt. For God has promised: 'my word that goes out from my mouth . . . will not return to me empty, but will accomplish what I desire and achieve the purpose for which I sent it' (Isaiah 55:11). Or the promise of the Lord Jesus: 'I will build my church; and the gates of hell shall not prevail against it' (Matthew 16:18 AV). With promises like that to stand on, all true ministers of the gospel have every reason to believe in the validity and worthwhileness of what they are doing, and to see their ministry as the greatest thing a man can do. Ours may be a day of 'small things', but we can be confident that God will ultimately accomplish all that he has promised in Christ Jesus.

## She lost what she loved most

The birth of a son was such an unexpected blessing that it must have brought the Shunammite and her husband closer together as husband and wife and also closer to God. All went well for a few years and the boy grew healthy and strong; but then suddenly disaster struck.

> The child grew, and one day he went out to his father, who was with the reapers. 'My head! My head!' he said to his father. His father told a servant, 'Carry him to his mother.' After the servant had lifted him up and carried him to his mother, the boy sat on her lap until noon, and then he died. She went up and laid him on the bed of the man of God, then shut the door and went out (2 Kings 4:18-21).

We can hardly imagine the feelings of this mother as she nursed her child and watched his life ebb away. If ever there was a time for bitterness of spirit and anger towards God this must surely have been it. It was almost as if her original objection to Elisha—'No, my lord . . . don't mislead your servant'—was being borne out, except that now it was God himself who seemed to be misleading her. He had given her the precious gift of a son to be loved and cherished with the expectation of years of future happiness, and now after a brief period he had taken that gift from her. The question we naturally ask is: Would it not have been better if the gift had not been given in the first place?

And that is a question that arises in other ways. On occasions God asks us to give up what we cherish most in this life and is the source of great personal happiness. It happened with Abraham.

> Then God said, 'Take your son, your only son, Isaac, whom you love, and go to the region of Moriah. Sacrifice him there as a burnt offering on one of the mountains I will tell you about' (Genesis 22:2).

Abraham must have asked himself why God would take away what had been given in fulfilment of his promise and had brought such great happiness to the lives of himself and Sarah. Could it have been, we wonder, that Abraham had been in danger of loving their one and only son more than he loved God? Was this what God wanted to teach both the Shunammite and Abraham, since in both instances, the lesson once learned, the child was restored?

We can all expose ourselves, quite unknowingly, to the temptation of loving someone or something that brings us great happiness and satisfaction more than we love God. We do not intend that it should be so, but the object of our affection quietly occupies the high ground in our hearts, and God has to compete in order to get his rightful place in our lives. And that is something God will not tolerate. That was exactly his complaint against the believers in the church at Ephesus. In spite of their hard work and perseverance, the risen Christ had to say to them: 'Yet I hold this against you: You have forsaken your first love' (Revelation 2:4). In a sermon upon the words of Hosea, 'Grey hairs are here and there upon him, yet he knoweth not', Robert Murray M'Cheyne makes the point that whilst the life of God in the soul cannot die, it is nevertheless liable to wither and decay. He then goes on:

This decay is always secret and unnoticed. It is like to the approach of old age. Old people never observe the gradual advance of old age. In general they do not like to think of their getting older. So it is in the decay of a believer's soul. It goes on secretly and silently: the eye of faith becomes dimmer and dimmer, the hand loses its firm hold of Jesus, the soul loses its fresh delight in Immanuel's finished work: and yet he knows it not. Sinful compliances steal upon the soul.

When that happens to us, God will sometimes, as with the Shunammite, shock us into the awareness of its happening by taking away what has claimed our first love and dethroned him from the central place in our hearts.

## She exercised great faith

The death of her child must have been a devastating blow to the Shunammite woman, and yet we do not read a single word of complaint or bitterness on her part towards God. On the contrary the tragedy seems only to have activated her faith. 'She called her husband and said, "Please send me one of the servants and a donkey so I can go to the man of God quickly and return"' (2 Kings 4:22). When Elisha saw her approaching he sent Gehazi to find out what had happened, but she brushed his questions aside and made straight for the prophet himself, falling at his feet in great distress (2 Kings 4:27). Elisha realised what had happened and gave his staff to Gehazi with instructions to run ahead to the house and lay the staff on the boy's face. But the Shunammite insisted that he himself as God's servant should accompany her back to the child. 'But the child's mother said, "As surely as the LORD lives and as you live, I will not leave you." So he got up and followed her' (2 Kings 4:30).

All this shows us her sense of priorities and the reality of her faith. She knew that the power of life and death lay with God alone in the person of his servant Elisha, and she was not satisfied with secondary agencies such as Gehazi or the prophet's staff. And she was right, because it was only God's power working through Elisha himself that brought the child back to life.

> When Elisha reached the house, there was the boy lying dead on his couch. He went in, shut the door on the two of them and prayed to the LORD. Then he got on the bed and lay upon the boy, mouth to mouth, eyes to eyes, hands to hands. As he stretched himself out upon him, the boy's body grew warm . . . The boy sneezed seven times and opened his eyes (2 Kings 4:32-35).

Our faith, if it is to do things for us and be the real strength of our lives, must not be centred in secondary agencies, however good they are in themselves. It is not our church membership, or baptism, or the Lord's table, or our good works, or anything else that we may trust in, but God alone. He is the source of grace and power in the Lord Jesus Christ.

# 21
# Hezekiah
## who revived the Church

*Read 2 Kings 18:1-6 and 2 Chronicles 29:1-11*

We know a great deal about king Hezekiah, since his reign is recorded in considerable detail in a total of eleven chapters in the books of Kings, Chronicles and Isaiah. The name Hezekiah means 'Jehovah is Strength', and he proved the truth of that in his own life, for he was not only a good king but a godly man. During his long reign of twenty-nine years he had many wonderful experiences, not the least of which was the fact that God used him to bring about a much needed revival of true worship among his people.

## His character

Simply because he was a king we may feel that Hezekiah had the kind of start in life the rest of us might envy. But that was not so. His father Ahaz was one of the most wicked kings in Judah's history, and during his reign the religious life of the nation reached an all-time low.

Ahaz was twenty years old when he became king . . . he did not do what was right in the eyes of the LORD his God. He walked in the ways of the kings of Israel and even sacrificed his son in the fire, following the detestable ways of the nations the LORD had driven out before the Israelites. He offered sacrifices and burned incense at the high

places, on the hilltops and under every spreading tree
(2 Kings 16:2-4).

With a father and a background like that, we may wonder
how Hezekiah became such a noble, spiritually minded man,
and the instrument in the hands of God for bringing about a
much needed revival in the Church in his day.

> Hezekiah . . . was twenty-five years old when he became
> king, and he reigned in Jerusalem for twenty-nine years
> . . . Hezekiah trusted in the LORD, the God of Israel. There
> was no-one like him among all the kings of Judah, either
> before him or after him. He held fast to the LORD and did
> not cease to follow him; he kept the commands the LORD
> had given Moses (2 Kings 18:1-2,5-6).

Where did his faith in God and his spiritual character
come from? Certainly not from his home background, as we
have seen. It can only have been that God's Spirit had
worked directly in his life, disturbing his conscience by the
depravity of the times and awakening in his heart a great
love for God and his Word. Not all have the blessing of being
brought up in a godly home, and in surroundings where the
gospel of Christ is taught and lived out, and prayer, the reading of God's Word and worship are normal activities. Therefore it is a great encouragement to know that, whereas God
will use any and every means to make his presence known in
a person's life, he does not ultimately depend upon any
external circumstances to bring someone into the understanding of salvation.

But Hezekiah did have one man who served as his spiritual
mentor and guide and who had a great influence on him from
the time he became king—the great prophet and preacher
Isaiah (Isaiah 37). Even so the prophet's voice seems to have

been a lonely one speaking for truth and righteousness in that godless age, and Hezekiah is to be commended for listening to him. There are many voices speaking in the world today: the philosopher and humanist with their doubts and uncertainties concerning truth, the modern theologians with the destructive criticism of the Bible, the politicians with their failed promises, the psychologists and psychiatrists who explain sin and wrongdoing in ways which deny personal responsibility, the educationalists for whom the answer to the ills of the world is to be found in yet more knowledge. But what is needed more and more for the well-being and salvation of mankind today is for kings, leaders and people to listen to the voice of God. Hezekiah 'held fast to the Lord and did not cease to follow him; he kept the commands the Lord had given Moses. And the Lord was with him . . .' (2 Kings 18:6-7).

## Demolition before construction

As a God-fearing man Hezekiah was anxious to get on with the work of constructing or reconstructing the spiritual life of the nation. He had great plans in mind for the temple and the priesthood and for the restoration of the Passover and the other great festivals of the Church which had been so long neglected. But first the ground had to be prepared and a work of demolition put in hand both spiritually and physically.

He removed the high places, smashed the sacred stones and cut down the Asherah poles. He broke into pieces the bronze snake Moses had made, for up to that time the Israelites had been burning incense to it. (It was called Nehushtan.)' (2 Kings 18:4).

This work of demolishing and sweeping away the pagan altars and idols in various parts of the country must not be interpreted as an act of religious and cultural vandalism. It was both right and necessary, and by it Hezekiah was showing that God totally rejected the false worship that had been going on for generations among his own people, and that it represented a clean break by the nation from its past, from the old life, the old ways and habits. It reminds us of God's terms of reference to Jeremiah when he called him into the work of the prophetic office. 'See, today I appoint you over nations and kingdoms to uproot and tear down, to destroy and overthrow, to build and to plant' (Jeremiah 1:10). Demolition was to precede construction.

The underlying principle here can be applied at the personal level. A similar work of demolition and sweeping away has to take place in a person's life before the positive work of salvation is experienced. There has to be repentance, and a turning away from reliance upon the old sinful self to total dependence upon what Christ has accomplished for us through his death on the cross. The old self is demolished, crucified with Christ, as Paul puts it, and a new self is born (constructed) within us by the power of God's Spirit. The new life in Christ is not simply a renovation of the old, in the way an old building is renovated to make it look new. In terms of salvation that would be no more than a personal moral reformation, and that is not what the gospel is about. Salvation is a twofold work in the heart carried out by the Holy Spirit, a work of total demolition and construction, of dying to sin and rising to new life in Christ. Paul puts it so well when he says: 'Therefore, if anyone is in Christ, he is a new creation; the old has gone, the new has come!' (2 Corinthians 5:17).

## Opening the doors

In the second part of our reading we come to the next phase in Hezekiah's reign. With the work of clearing out idol worship

from the land well under way, he next turned his attention to
the task of reviving the spiritual life of the nation. The worship of God's house had been neglected during the reign of
Ahaz and the temple building itself closed.

> Ahaz gathered together the furnishings from the temple
> of God and took them away. He shut the doors of the
> LORD's temple and set up altars at every street corner in
> Jerusalem (2 Chronicles 28:24).

One of Hezekiah's first acts was to throw open the doors of
the house of God and let in not only the light of day but the
light of truth.

> In the first month of the first year of his reign, he opened
> the doors of the temple of the LORD and repaired them. He
> brought in the priests and the Levites, assembled them in
> the square on the east side and said, 'Listen to me, Levites!
> Consecrate yourselves now and consecrate the temple of
> the LORD, the God of your fathers. Remove all defilement
> from the sanctuary. Our fathers were unfaithful; they did
> evil in the eyes of the LORD our God and forsook him.
> They turned their faces away from the LORD's dwelling-
> place and turned their backs on him. They also shut the
> doors of the portico and put out the lamps. They did not
> burn incense or present any burnt offerings at the sanctu-
> ary to the God of Israel' (2 Chronicles 29:3-7).

So Hezekiah began the work of renewing and reviving the
services of the house of God. By opening the doors of the
temple he was calling the people back to prayer and worship; this was a priority if the power of God was to move
again in the land. And that remains true in every age. True

revival begins with the Church and the people of God. We have a wonderful promise given by God himself:

> If my people, who are called by my name, will humble themselves and pray and seek my face and turn from their wicked ways, then will I hear from heaven and will forgive their sin and will heal their land (2 Chronicles 7:14).

But it must begin with the Church, God's people who are called by his name. The people of Judah in Hezekiah's time were unfaithful and had strayed far from God, but they were still his people in whom he desired a revival of prayer and worship and spiritual life. God was not concerned with reviving the surrounding pagan nations but his own people, the Church. Hezekiah was aware of this and made his first act the opening of the doors of the temple and the restoration of its worship and priesthood.

Revival can come to a local church as well as to the whole Church. Every fellowship needs to be revived from time to time because we can so easily become listless and apathetic in our worship and praise. Peter says, 'For it is time for judgment to begin with the family of God' (1 Peter 4:17). He means, among other things, that God's people need to go through a refining process from time to time, and this can be painful. Old habits and old allegiances may need cleansing and old grievances may need healing before the Spirit comes in reviving power.

## A personal covenant with God

Hezekiah was aware of the enormity of the task which faced him and to which he was called, and therefore he entered into a personal covenant with God. 'I intend to make a covenant with the LORD, the God of Israel, so that his fierce anger will turn away from us' (2 Chronicles 29:10).

Once started on the work of reformation and renewal, Hezekiah threw himself into it with a tremendous sense of zeal and dedication. He called the priests together and addressed them as follows: 'My sons, do not be negligent now, for the LORD has chosen you to stand before him and serve him, to minister before him and to burn incense' (v.11). He re-instituted the sacrificial system of worship in the temple:

> Hezekiah gave the order to sacrifice the burnt offering on the altar. As the offering began, singing to the LORD began also, accompanied by trumpets and the instruments of David king of Israel. The whole assembly bowed in worship . . . (vv.27-28).

He sent messengers throughout the country calling the people back to God.

> At the king's command, couriers went throughout Israel and Judah with letters . . . which read: 'People of Israel, return to the LORD, the God of Abraham, Isaac and Israel, that he may return to you . . . ' (2 Chronicles 30:6).

To accomplish all this and to turn the tide of popular religious feeling back from the idolatry that had swept over the nation in the reign of Ahaz was an enormous undertaking, calling for great courage and unshakeable faith on Hezekiah's part. Hence his need to enter into a personal covenant with God so that his strength would not fail.

We are living in difficult times where the Christian faith is concerned, and we all find our strength and zeal flagging at times. Pastors get downhearted and discouraged when, in spite of all their hard work and fervent preaching, they see few conversions, congregations remain small and the gospel seems to have minimal impact upon the local community.

For those working in inner-city areas the temptation to discouragement is all the greater when, in addition to the coldness of people's hearts towards the things of God, there is the problem of vandalism and the sheer ugliness and desolation of areas full of decaying buildings, and spaces littered with broken-down cars and the rubbish of modern urban living. The ordinary Christian too can find it a lonely and discouraging business to be the only one with a concern for spiritual matters in the place of work, the home, the school or college. For ours is an age that militates against holiness of life and has absorbed into its system the so-called progressive ideas of humanistic thinking—sexual permissiveness, easier divorce, abortion on demand, homosexuality as an alternative lifestyle, free access to pornography, shorter prison sentences for serious crime, the lowering of the age of consent, longer drinking hours, the legalisation of drugs, voluntary euthanasia, etc.

Is it possible to turn the tide of such thinking? God can do it. Hezekiah's reign proves that. 'Hezekiah and all the people rejoiced at what God had brought about for his people, because it was done so quickly' (2 Chronicles 29:36). But how do we keep going in the meantime? How do we keep up our courage, and keep our spiritual zeal from flagging? Hezekiah points the way in this too, through his entering into a personal covenant with God. He reminded himself that he was God's man on the throne, called to serve him in a crisis situation, and that that called for renewed commitment and rededication on his part.

So it is with us. We are God's covenant people, and we need to keep renewing that covenant at the personal level. We are living in a day of spiritual crisis; this is no time to look for a Christian lifestyle that is easy, comfortable, laid-back and without challenge, cost or sacrifice. To quote A. W.

Tozer, we are not to think of this world as a 'playground' but as a 'battleground'. We must ask ourselves: Is that what Christ has called me to—an easy laid-back Christianity? Is there not a cross at the heart of our Christian faith, a cross on which the Son of God died to save me? Should I be content then to give nothing back in return?

# 22
# Hezekiah
## the man of action and prayer

*Read 2 Chronicles 32:1-8 and Isaiah 37:1-20*

In these two passages we learn something of the way in which king Hezekiah acted in a crisis situation. We all have to face crisis of one kind or another at some time in our lives, and it helps to know how other people face up to it, especially if they have faith in God. The crisis for Hezekiah was of a political nature. 'After all that Hezekiah had so faithfully done, Sennacherib king of Assyria came and invaded Judah. He laid siege to the fortified cities, thinking to conquer them for himself' (2 Chronicles 32:1-2). This was no empty threat, since the Assyrian war-machine had a reputation for brutality and conquest known far and wide. Byron in his poem 'The Destruction of Sennacherib' gives us some idea of the fear the mighty Assyrian army struck into the hearts of smaller nations.

> The Assyrian came down like the wolf on the fold,
> And his cohorts were gleaming in purple and gold;
> And the sheen of their spears was like stars on the sea,
> When the blue wave rolls nightly on deep Galilee.

How did Hezekiah respond to this situation? He did so in two ways, at the practical and spiritual levels.

## The practical level

We have already seen that Hezekiah was a man with a strong faith in the power of God to change things. But we would be quite wrong to suppose that he was some kind of starry-eyed idealist who depended on God always to intervene in miraculous ways. Not at all. He was a very down-to-earth practical man who believed that God helps those who help themselves. In the face of the Assyrian aggression he acted very promptly and efficiently, showing himself to be a man of action and a true leader of his people.

> When Hezekiah saw that Sennacherib had come and that he intended to make war on Jerusalem, he consulted with his officials and military staff about blocking off the water from the springs outside the city . . . 'Why should the kings of Assyria come and find plenty of water?' they said. Then he worked hard repairing all the broken sections of the wall and building towers on it. He built another wall outside that one and reinforced the supporting terraces . . . He also made large numbers of weapons and shields.
>
> He appointed military officers over the people and assembled them before him in the square . . . and encouraged them with these words: 'Be strong and courageous. Do not be afraid . . . of the king of Assyria and the vast army with him, for there is a greater power with us than with him. With him is only the arm of flesh, but with us is the LORD our God to help us and to fight our battles' (2 Chronicles 32:2-8).

When it comes to facing the critical situations of life we must never lose sight of the fact that there is always God's part and there is our part as well. We shall see shortly that

Hezekiah in his distress looked to God for help, but this did not mean that there was no input he could make at the practical level. He didn't simply wait for divine intervention. He did everything he possibly could at the practical and military level to counter the Assyrian threat. The story of Peter's escape from prison in Acts 12 is a good example of this principle at work.

> Suddenly an angel of the LORD appeared and a light shone in the cell. He struck Peter on the side and woke him up. 'Quick, get up!' he said, and the chains fell off Peter's wrists. Then the angel said to him, 'Put on your clothes and sandals . . . Wrap your cloak around you and follow me' (Acts 12:7,8).

God did not do miraculously for Peter what Peter could do for himself. Only the intervention of God's power could overcome the problem of the sentries and break the chains that held Peter fast. But Peter could put on his own clothes and sandals and wrap himself in his cloak and follow the angel. We have our human limitations, and there are situations that face us in this life which we can do nothing about and which become a test of our faith. But what we *can* do we *must* do. God expects it of us and has given us certain powers and energy and sanctified common sense which we are to use to help ourselves.

## The spiritual level

Hezekiah was well aware of the disastrous situation facing him and of the limitations of his own attempts to deal with it. He was not being melodramatic therefore when in our second passage, Isaiah 37:1, we read: 'When King Hezekiah heard this, he tore his clothes and put on sackcloth and went into the temple of the LORD.' In addition he sent messengers to Isaiah the prophet to request his prayers.

> This is what Hezekiah says: This day is a day of distress and rebuke and disgrace . . . It may be that the LORD your God will hear the words of the field commander, whom his master, the king of Assyria, has sent to ridicule the living God . . . Therefore pray for the remnant that still survives (Isaiah 37:3-4).

But he doesn't stop there. When a letter from the king of Assyria arrives setting out the terms of surrender, Hezekiah knows that talking with his officials or even with the prophet Isaiah is not enough—he has to talk with God directly. 'Hezekiah received the letter from the messengers and read it. Then he went up to the temple of the LORD and spread it out before the LORD. And Hezekiah prayed to the LORD' (Isaiah 37:14-15).

What a graphic picture of man's dependence upon God in the face of life's crisis—the king on his knees spreading out the letter and his need before God! Some would commend Hezekiah for the practical and military steps taken earlier, but would regard what he was now doing in the temple as a pointless exercise. What hope has prayer in the face of the Assyrian war-machine? A little child has more chance of stopping a ten-ton truck. But there are those of us who from our own experience know better. In our critical situations we have known how good it is to have friends to talk with and share the burden, and who have given us wise advice and comfort. But with the best will in the world they haven't always been able to enter into the depth of the situation. Like ourselves, their powers are limited and there is no more they can do. That is the point at which we have had to go beyond ourselves and beyond friends and counsellors and, like Hezekiah, we have spread it out before the Lord and said in effect, 'Lord, this is a desperate situation I am in and only you can help me.'

For the Christian believer there ought to be a perfect naturalness about this talking things through with God. It ought not to be irksome, and yet for some prayer is exactly that—it is something we are reluctant to start and glad to finish. C. S. Lewis raises the important question why it is that, within the discipline of the Church, prayer is set as a penance. He suggests it is because we tend to regard prayer as a tiresome duty rather than a joy and a refreshment to our souls. When that lovely winsome character, Billy Bray the Cornish evangelist, was asked to make some decision or other, he was fond of saying, 'Well, I'll have to talk to the Father about it.' It was the most natural thing in the world for him to spread all his concerns before the Lord. That is what Hezekiah did.

## Hezekiah's prayer

The prayer itself is deeply instructive and there is much we can learn from it.

Hezekiah begins in the first place with God and his greatness, not with himself and his crisis situation. 'O LORD Almighty, God of Israel, enthroned between the cherubim, you alone are God over all the kingdoms of the earth. You have made heaven and earth' (Isaiah 37:16). It is a time of national crisis and, anxious as he is to spread his request before God, he does not forget to give God his rightful place in the worship and adoration due to him. That is true of all the great prayers of the Bible; they begin with acknowledging God for who he is in himself, and only then do the requests follow for help and guidance. And that is how it should be. We said earlier that there is a naturalness about talking things through with God, but that doesn't mean that we should be irreverent or overfamiliar and look upon prayer simply as an automatic device for getting the things we want.

The Lord Jesus makes that perfectly clear in the model prayer he has given us. It begins with God, not with ourselves or our problems. 'Our Father who art in heaven, hallowed by Thy name.' God is in heaven: we are on earth; he is infinite: we are finite; he is the Creator: we are the creatures. To hallow God's name is to hold God in reverence because of who he is, the Holy and Eternal One. And it is only after we have given God our worship and adoration in this way that we are to bring before him our personal needs for daily bread etc.

Second, Hezekiah was deeply concerned for God's glory. 'Give ear, O LORD, and hear; open your eyes, O LORD, and see; listen to all the words Sennacherib has sent to insult the living God' (v.17). As he sees it, the honour of God is at stake, and it disturbs him. Sennacherib had shown a total contempt for God, and had ridiculed and blasphemed God's name by claiming that he was no greater or more powerful than the gods of the surrounding pagan nations. 'Do not let Hezekiah mislead you when he says, "The LORD will deliver us." Has the god of any nation ever delivered his land from the hand of the king of Assyria? Where are the gods of Hamath and Arpad? Where are the gods of Sepharvaim? Have they rescued Samaria from my hand?' (Isaiah 36:18-19). Hezekiah is outraged that the eternal God, the maker 'of heaven and earth', should be reduced to the level of an idol. He longs therefore for God to vindicate his honour and to reveal his glory and power through the deliverance of Jerusalem.

Are we concerned for God's glory? Does it disturb and hurt us when we hear the name of Christ being blasphemed on TV and when God's laws and commandments are treated with contempt? Do we long for God to vindicate his name and his gospel in the world? If it does not disturb us unduly, or fill us with a deep anger and righteous indignation, when we see all that is holy and true being ridiculed and scorned in this way, then it is an ominous sign that something profound is happening within us. It means that we are being insidiously moulded and shaped by the world's thinking and values, and that we are imbibing the current philosophy of the age into our system. Let us be alert therefore and remain sensitive where God's glory is concerned.

Third, he acknowledges and affirms God's sovereignty in the history of men and nations.

> It is true, O Lord, that the Assyrian kings have laid waste all these peoples and their lands. They have thrown their gods into the fire and destroyed them, for they were not gods but only wood and stone, fashioned by human hands. Now, O Lord our God, deliver us from his hand, so that all kingdoms on earth may know that you alone, O Lord, are God (Isaiah 37:18-20).

The idol gods of the pagan nations had failed to save them in the time of crisis, and Sennacherib was counting on the same thing happening to Jerusalem because of the failure of the God of Israel to do anything about it. But Hezekiah believes otherwise.

The pagan gods were the product of men's hands, whereas the God of Israel is Lord over all the kingdoms of the earth. He alone is the true God and he is the One who is ultimately shaping the affairs of men and nations and working

out his eternal purposes in history. It is not human governments or tyrants like Sennacherib, or the power politics of
this world, that guide things to their final outcome, but God
himself. The forces of sin and of Satan, working through men
and governments in opposition to the gospel of Christ's
kingdom by persecution and repression, through spiritual
indifference and man's greed and violence, may frustrate
God's purpose for a time, but always they have ended by
being shattered on the rock of God's judgment. We have
seen it happen in our own day with the forces of Communism, and so it was with Sennacherib.

> Then the angel of the LORD went out and put to death a
> hundred and eighty-five thousand men in the Assyrian
> camp . . . So Sennacherib king of Assyria broke camp and
> withdrew . . . One day, while he was worshipping in the
> temple of his god Nisroch, his sons Adrammelech and
> Sharezer cut him down with the sword . . . (Isaiah 37:36-38).

Nothing can ultimately frustrate the purpose of God from
pressing forward to that final day, when, at the coming of the
Lord Jesus, the kingdom of this world will become the kingdom of our God and of his Christ (Revelation 11:15).

# 23
# Daniel
## the young man who wouldn't
## be brainwashed

*Read Daniel 1*

In the opening chapter of the book of Daniel we are not only introduced to the man himself, but we also learn something of the background to the captivity of the Jewish people in Babylon.

> In the third year of the reign of Jehoiakim king of Judah, Nebuchadnezzar king of Babylon came to Jerusalem and besieged it. And the Lord delivered Jehoiakim king of Judah into his hand, along with some of the articles from the temple of God. These he carried off to . . . Babylonia and put in the treasure-house of his god (Daniel 1:1-2).

We may wonder, in the first place, why God allowed his people to be exiled in a foreign land. The answer is because of Judah's sin and disobedience, and her willingness to be influenced by the idolatry of the surrounding pagan nations instead of seeking to influence them. God had warned Judah again and again of his coming judgment, and eventually it came in the form of Nebuchadnezzar's conquest and the captivity of the people. There were three deportations to Babylon, and Daniel was in the first—mentioned above—which took place in 605 BC. The last occurred in 586 BC when Nebuchadnezzar destroyed Jerusalem and its temple.

Daniel is a truly great and outstanding figure. He is described by Ezekiel as a man of extraordinary wisdom and righteousness (Ezekiel 14:14). The Lord Jesus also mentions Daniel in connection with a prophecy about the fall of Jerusalem (Matthew 24:15). Daniel was a prophet and statesman who served in high office in Babylon during the reigns of Nebuchadnezzar, Belshazzar, Darius and Cyrus. He came from a royal or noble family background and remained in Babylon for the whole of the period of exile, lasting seventy years, by which time he must have been an old man.

## The policy of assimilation

In all probability Daniel was no more than a teenager, perhaps sixteen or seventeen, when he arrived in Babylon with the first deportation. Because of his noble background he and other members of the nobility were given special treatment.

> Then the king ordered Ashpenaz, chief of his court officials, to bring in some of the Israelites from the royal family and the nobility—young men without any physical defect, handsome, showing aptitude for every kind of learning, well informed, quick to understand, and qualified to serve in the king's palace . . . Among these were some from Judah: Daniel, Hananiah, Mishael and Azariah (Daniel 1:3,4,6).

All this was deliberate policy on the part of Nebuchadnezzar, who was building up his empire by subjugating different peoples. He realised that he could best keep them in submission by assimilating some of their leading families into the life and culture of Babylon. The chief official,

Ashpenaz, 'was to teach them the language and literature of the Babylonians. The king assigned them a daily amount of food and wine from the king's table. They were to be trained for three years, and after that they were to enter the king's service' (vv.4,5). Even their names were to be changed from Jewish to Babylonian. 'The chief official gave them new names: to Daniel, the name Belteshazzar; to Hananiah, Shadrach; to Mishael, Meshach; and to Azariah, Abednego' (Daniel 1:7). These were all names connected with the Babylonian gods. It was Nebuchnezzar's aim, through this process of indoctrination or brainwashing, to change the way these young men would think and behave, by putting every thought of God out of their minds. They were to become pagans, adopting pagan names and imbibing a pagan culture.

In the world of politics we have seen this brainwashing technique being used in our own time in Russia, China and Cuba, where Communist indoctrination through posters, slogans, and political classes held in factories, schools and offices, has attempted to wash clean from people's mind any other political persuasion but the teachings of Communism. But even more serious from the spiritual standpoint is the subtle brainwashing that goes on all the time—through TV, films, newspapers and magazines, advertising and the pop culture—to obliterate from people's minds any trace of godliness and Christian morality and to supplant it with the atheistic values of secular humanism. And all too often people, including Christian believers, are not aware of this process taking place and how it is changing their patterns of thinking and behaviour. But we need to be aware of it, and to be on our guard, because we can so easily become infected by this worldly spirit and all too readily drift into an acceptance of its values and conventions.

## Daniel's first stand

Young though he was, Daniel realised what was happening
and what the king's intentions were, and he was immediately on his guard. 'But Daniel resolved not to defile himself
with the royal food and wine, and he asked the chief official
for permission not to defile himself in this way' (Daniel 1:8).
That word 'resolved' is important since it suggests a strong
sense of conviction on Daniel's part. He was determined to
make a stand against the brainwashing process. There were
three things distinctly pagan in character he had to reckon
with. First, the learning, culture and language of Babylon.
Second, his pagan name. Third, the eating of the king's food.
It seems strange on the face of it that it was against the last of
these, the food and drink which in itself was such a trivial
thing, that Daniel chose to make his stand. Why was that?

The answer is that accepting the language and culture and
being given a pagan name were not things that involved any
conscientious scruples as a child of God. Learning the language of Babylon would be of great help to him, and accepting its culture and learning didn't mean he had to accept
everything he was taught. After all, Moses was 'educated in
all the wisdom of the Egyptians' (Acts 7:22), which equipped
him to understand the Egyptian mind better in his contest
with Pharaoh. As to his pagan name, although it was intended
to symbolise that he had given up all thoughts of God, that
was not how he felt within his heart and mind. But eating the
king's food was quite a different matter. This was not a
minor issue, as we might think, but it was a fundamental
challenge to Daniel's faith in the true God, and thus something on which he was resolved to make his stand. The feasts
at the king's table were dedicated to the Babylonian gods,
and before the food was eaten part of it would have been

sacrificed to some idol or other. So to share in it would have meant recognising the principle of idolatry and denying the worship of the only true God. That is what Daniel meant when we read that he resolved not to 'defile' himself with the king's food. The food therefore was not a trivial matter, but basic to Daniel's faith and convictions, so he had to make a stand.

There are certain things we can learn from this. First, like Daniel, Christians need to discern between the things about which we need have no spiritual scruples, and those things on which we cannot compromise and we must make a stand. We must be careful not to make ourselves offensive by our own stubbornness and narrowness of outlook and thus pro-voke unnecessary opposition. We need to keep in mind our Lord's words: 'Blessed are you when people insult you, per-secute you and falsely say all kinds of evil against you because of me' (Matthew 5:11). The key phrase is 'because of me', and not because of our own narrowness and stupidity or offensive manner.

Second, the phrase 'But Daniel resolved' is really the key to understanding his character and the faith that enabled him to withstand seventy years in exile in Babylon, with all its glittering materialism, without denying his God. As a youngster of inflexible principle he was already showing all the signs of the man of 'granite character' he would later become. This kind of spiritual and moral strength is all too rare these days, even among Christian men. Part of the explanation lies in the unisex philosophy of today which minimises the manliness of men and their leadership role in the home and society. This is not to deny that women too need spiritual and moral strength. But the Word of God teaches quite categorically that if men are to fulfil their lead-ership role in the family, the church and the nation, then they need to be men of resolve and purpose who do not opt out of leadership roles, as happens all too often in church and family life.

## Honoured by God

Daniel's resolve and integrity of character certainly made a favourable impression upon the king's chief official. 'Now God had caused the official to show favour and sympathy to Daniel' (v.9). We should not forget that God watches over his servants and moves the minds and hearts of men for the good of his own children. Things do not happen haphazardly in this world; not to those who believe in the sovereignty of God and the mysteriousness of his ways with men. But the official was now put on the spot, since he dared not disobey the king's command. So we read:

> Daniel then said . . . 'Please test your servants for ten days. Give us nothing but vegetables to eat and water to drink. Then compare our appearance with that of the young men who eat the royal food' . . . At the end of ten days they looked healthier and better nourished than any of the young men who ate the royal food. So the guard took away their choice food . . . and gave them vegetables instead (vv.11-16).

Daniel and his friends came through the test successfully, for God honoured the stand he made; and therefore Daniel and his friends could look to God to honour them in the future, even when it came to the lions' den and the fiery furnace. From one perspective the king's food was a little thing to risk getting into trouble about, but Daniel knew if he couldn't stand for the little thing, then he certainly wouldn't be able to stand on a big issue like the lions' den. Our Lord's parable of the talents teaches the same lesson: 'Well done, good and faithful servant! You have been faithful with a few things; I will put you in charge of many things' (Matthew 25:21). If a man is unfaithful and irresponsible in the minor things of life, then God cannot trust him to carry out the big tasks.

In the New Testament Stephen is a good example of this principle at work. He was a prominent leader and preacher in the early church and the first Christian martyr. But he did not begin in a high position. His first job was to 'wait on tables' (Acts 6), and it was only as his faithfulness and gifts became increasingly recognised that his work expanded into preaching and evangelising. He proved himself in the low position and God moved him up higher.

## Developing our potential for God

The training of Daniel and his friends in the language, litera-ture and general culture of Babylon lasted three years. They were clearly young men of high intelligence and natural ability, 'showing aptitude for every kind of learning, well informed, quick to understand' (Daniel 1:4). But there was more to their training than natural ability, since we are told that God himself helped them to develop their potential to an exceptional degree: 'To these four young men God gave knowledge and understanding of all kinds of literature and learning. And Daniel could understand visions and dreams of all kinds' (v.17). Although we are not told in any great detail what kind of students they were, or what particular subjects they studied, they must have worked really hard, because when the period of training came to an end and they were taken before the king, he was more than satisfied with their progress, and they entered into his service.

At the end of the time set by the king to bring them in, the chief official presented them to Nebuchadnezzar. The king talked with them, and he found none equal to Daniel, Hananiah, Mishael and Azariah; so they entered the king's service. In every matter of wisdom and understanding . . . he found them ten times better than all the magicians and enchanters in his whole kingdom (vv.18-20).

Daniel and his friends worked and studied hard because they had a sense of spiritual responsibility, and were prepared to equip themselves mentally in readiness to serve God in any way he might choose for them in the future. All of us have gifts and abilities of one kind or another, and maximising their potential in the service of God is our own personal responsibility. The parable of the talents mentioned earlier (Matthew 25:14-30) ends with the words: 'For everyone who has will be given more, and he will have an abundance. Whoever does not have, even what he has will be taken from him.' That is surely saying that when we put our natural endowments at the disposal of God he will help us develop them and impart to us other gifts and abilities, as he did with Daniel and his friends. The power of the Holy Spirit does this, imparting wisdom, understanding and insight into the things of God. He brings to light in us abilities and hidden potential we may never have realised we possessed. But, like Daniel and his friends, we must be open to God's leading, believing that he can use us in his service, however great or small our gift or talent may be.

The reverse of all this is also true. Our Lord's words, 'Whoever does not have, even what he has will be taken from him' (Matthew 25:29), are a warning that if we do not fulfil our potential by using the opportunities and abilities we have for glorifying God, then they may be taken from us. That was the sin of the man with one talent in our Lord's parable. He did nothing with it, but 'hid [it] in the ground'. He despised the little ability and opportunity he had and didn't think it worth developing. We do not all have the same abilities and gifts, and therefore we do not all have the same opportunity to serve God. But although we cannot all be equal in what we achieve for God, we can be equal in the effort we put into it. The  level of potential we possess is in God's hands, and therefore the only question that will count at the judgment day will be: 'Have we fulfilled the potential given to us?'

# 24
# Daniel
## the statesman

*Read Daniel 6*

The years have rolled by and our present chapter opens with Daniel now an old man of eighty or more. He had been in public life for something like sixty years, and for a large part of that time had served the Babylonian Empire with great distinction, holding high office during the rule of Nebuchadnezzar. With the accession of Belshazzar to the throne there came a change in the style of government; corruption, luxury and licence now dominated public life. Little is heard of Daniel during this period until the very end of Belshazzar's reign, when he is called out of retirement to interpret the writing on the wall, spelling out the judgment of God upon Belshazzar and the defeat of his kingdom by Darius, the ruler of the Medes and Persians, with whom chapter six opens.

## Politics and religion

With the accession of Darius, Daniel is once again given an opportunity to exercise his gift of statesmanship in the affairs of the nation.

It pleased Darius to appoint 120 satraps to rule throughout the kingdom, with three administrators over them,

one of whom was Daniel. The satraps were made accountable to them so that the king might not suffer loss. Now
Daniel so distinguished himself among the administrators
and the satraps by his exceptional qualities that the king
planned to set him over the whole kingdom (Daniel 6:1-3).

It is evident that Darius regarded Daniel as a man of
unimpeachable integrity and a statesman of the first rank.
Indeed, so impressed is he with Daniel's contribution to
political life and the public good that he intends making him
his Prime Minister. Even Daniel's enemies recognised that,
unlike so many others in political and public life, he was
incorruptible and free of any kind of sleaze. 'They could find
no corruption in him, because he was trustworthy and neither corrupt nor negligent' (Daniel 6:4). Doesn't all this say
something to us about the relationship between Christianity
and politics, and the vital role believers can play in political
and public life? After all, we keep hearing today about the
'sleaze factor' in politics, so that it would act as a necessary
disinfectant to have more men and women of godly character like Daniel active in the political affairs of our nation.

Think for a moment of those men in the Bible whom God
used in such a powerful way in guiding the political affairs of
their own times. Joseph was Prime Minister in Egypt under
Pharaoh and saved the nation from destruction by famine.
Isaiah was not only a prophet but also an adviser in the courts
of Uzziah and Hezekiah. Nehemiah was the governor of Jerusalem under the Persian king Artaxerxes during the period
of restoration after the exile. In Acts 13 we hear of the conversion of the Roman proconsul Sergius Paulus under the preaching of Paul and Barnabas. What is more, our Lord Jesus had
something to say about our contribution to political life when
he answered the question about giving taxes to Caesar.

'Is it right to pay taxes to Caesar or not? Should we pay or shouldn't we?' But Jesus knew their hypocrisy. 'Why are you trying to trap me?' he asked, 'Bring me a denarius and let me look at it.' They brought the coin, and he asked them, 'Whose portrait is this? And whose inscription?' 'Caesar's', they replied. Then Jesus said to them, 'Give to Caesar what is Caesar's and to God what is God's' (Mark 12:14-17).

As citizens Christians must necessarily take an interest in decision-making at the political level, either actively, by adopting a role in national or local politics, or by the responsible use of their vote. Caesar has legitimate demands upon us through our taxes, service and obedience to the laws of the land. We must give to Caesar what rightly belongs to Caesar, because such government and authority come from God. 'Everyone must submit to the governing authorities, for there is no authority except that which God has established' (Romans 13:1). The existence of so much failure in leadership in our country today, and the frequent allegations of bribery, immorality and corruption in public and political life, go to show how far we have fallen as a nation from this biblical view of government and politics. We need godly men and women like Daniel to restore integrity and honesty and credibility to political and public life.

Furthermore, the Bible exhorts us to remember in our prayers those who have the responsibility for political leadership.

I urge, then, first of all, that requests, prayers, intercession and thanksgiving be made for everyone—for kings and all those in authority, that we may live peaceful and quiet lives in all godliness and holiness (1 Timothy 2:1-2).

We need to pray that those in positions of leadership in public life who give no thought to God, may change their ways and realise that their authority comes from God, as Jesus reminded Pilate (John 19:11), and that they are accountable to God. Likewise, we must especially pray for those in authority who are believers, that God may empower and strengthen them in the discharge of their public duties, as he did Daniel.

After all, we must not forget that whilst we are to give to Caesar what belongs to Caesar, our Lord also reminded us that we are to give to God what belongs to God. This can mean conflict between the demands of the state and the demands of God. Daniel was soon to face this dilemma with his elevation to chief administrator.

## The pressures of evil

Because he was a man of God, incorruptible and honest in his discharge of public affairs, Daniel's fellow administrators and the lesser officials were out to get him. They recognised that they could not fault him in the discharge of his office; they would only be able to discredit him through his faith in God. 'Finally these men said, "We will never find any basis for charges against this man Daniel unless it has something to do with the law of his God"' (Daniel 6:5).

This shows us the true nature of evil at work in the world; it constantly seeks to frustrate the purposes of God in the lives of believers. Daniel had done nothing wrong; he was not a cheat or a liar or incompetent. Yet his contemporaries in high office were determined to bring about his downfall, for no other reason than that he was a lover of God. Theirs was a perverse and totally irrational attitude, which can only be explained in terms of the Satanic influence at work in the power structures of the world system. Whenever a Christian believer is pressurised by evil men and women in the place of work, or in the home, or in public and political life, we must see it as a small part of that greater warfare that is constantly raging between the kingdom of truth and righteousness and the kingdom of evil and darkness.

This is the only way to understand and make sense of the crucifixion of our Lord. If the Lord Jesus had been a terrorist or a murderer or a man of evil and violence, then perhaps we could begin to understand why he was crucified. But he was none of these things. His life was one of pure goodness, love, and service to others. And yet they nailed him to a cross. Where is the sense or rationality in a perverse response like that to such a lovely life? There is only one explanation. It was the work of Satan and of sin in the hearts of men and women. And when we realise, further, that those who crucified our Lord shared the same human nature as we have, we are beginning really to know ourselves for the first time. We see human nature for what it is—perverse, corrupt and sinful. And only God's power can help us to do something about it. This is the essence of the gospel of Jesus Christ, that he—God's own Son—gave himself as a ransom for sin and to deliver us from the power and domination of Satan and the corruption of death.

## Daniel's dilemma

In dealing with the warfare of the Spirit the apostle Paul refers to what he calls 'the devil's schemes' (Ephesians 6:11). He means that the devil is very cunning in the way he attacks God's people. His is not always the direct frontal attack; sometimes he employs a much more subtle and devious strategy. This was the approach of Daniel's fellow officials.

By means of flattery and lying they appealed to the king's vanity and egotism, and especially to the fact that ancient kings were often regarded as gods or divine beings in their own right.

> So the administrators and the satraps went as a group to the king and said: 'O King Darius, live for ever! The royal administrators, prefects, satraps, advisers and governors have all agreed that the king should issue an edict and enforce the decree that anyone who prays to any god or man during the next thirty days, except to you, O king, shall be thrown into the lions' den' (Daniel 6:6,7).

Flattery, lies and deception are powerful weapons with Satan, and often succeed where the direct frontal assault fails. Sometimes he is 'like a roaring lion looking for someone to devour' (1 Peter 5:8), but at other times he 'masquerades as an angel of light' (2 Corinthians 11:14), appealing to our pride and vanity and human weakness. Immediately the king's decree was made known Daniel was faced with a most difficult dilemma. It was the Caesar and God syndrome of which the Lord Jesus spoke, and which faces all Christians from time to time in some form or other. Up to this point Daniel had given Caesar what rightly belonged to him, but now he had to give to God what belonged to God—his faith and trust and commitment. He knew his enemies were watching him to see which way he would turn, and he also knew the consequences of the choice he made to put God before Caesar.

This is a choice that confronts all God's people from time to time in the various situations of life. It enters the life of the Christian man or woman who holds high public office and whose conscience clashes with policy; it makes itself felt in the committee rooms of local government where Christian conviction challenges political expediency; it comes into the place of work where the believer has to decide whether to align himself or herself with greed and profit or with Christ and his truth; it enters the family where, for the sake of peace and harmony, the Christian parent is tempted to take the road of least resistance with the children rather than apply the principles of the gospel. These are all situations tied up with our place in the community as citizens and private individuals, and the dilemmas they pose call for all the courage and strength which Daniel showed and which only God himself can give us.

## What Daniel actually did

In his response to the king's decree Daniel did three things in particular which serve as an example to us and may help us when facing our own dilemmas.

First, he didn't hide his faith from the world.

> Now when Daniel learned that the decree had been published, he went home to his upstairs room where the windows opened towards Jerusalem. Three times a day he got down on his knees and prayed . . . (Daniel 6:10).

He didn't worship God in secret but deliberately kept his windows open so that all could see him at his devotions. It is not easy to make your faith in the Lord Jesus Christ public when you know that it makes you unpopular and brings down ridicule. The temptation can be very strong to keep the window of faith closed between us and the world, instead of throwing it wide open. But a secret faith is of little use in the long run. One of two things must happen. Either the secrecy will kill the faith, or the faith will kill the secrecy when, in boldness of the Holy Spirit, we open up to all the world to show to whom we belong.

Second, he showed he believed in the reality of prayer:

'Three times a day he got down on his knees and prayed'. What else could he do when faced with the awful dilemma that confronted him? No one else could help him, only God. It is in such situations that we begin to see that prayer is an essential ingredient of life's experience and not simply a devotional exercise we mechanically engage in. As the hymn rightly says, 'Prayer is the Christian's vital breath, the Christian's native air'. Is it *our* vital breath and native air? Is it the spiritual oxygen that breathes life into our soul? Do we really believe in the power of prayer in the way Daniel did?

Third, he showed that he was totally consistent in his spiritual life. 'Three times a day he got down on his knees and prayed, giving thanks to God, *just as he had done before.'* He didn't change his routine because his circumstances had changed. He did what he always did, whether the circumstances were good or bad. He simply went on consistently with his regular devotions and godly discipline. So often we can be spasmodic in our devotional life. We pray or keep our 'quiet time' when we 'feel like it'. We keep our devotional life going along steadily for a time; then something happens to change our circumstances—a death in the family perhaps, or serious illness, or some perplexing problem or difficulty that throws us off balance—and we begin to wilt, and prayer and the reading of God's Word and worship begin to falter. In short, we lack consistency. We live our Christian life in a series of fits and starts rather than steadily running with perseverance 'the race marked out for us' (Hebrews 12:1).

## Paying the price

Of course, if we are going to be as consistent in our faith in God as Daniel was in his, then like him we must be prepared to pay the price. For him it was the lions' den. 'So the king gave the order, and they brought Daniel and threw him into the lions' den' (v.16). True, God delivered him from the lions, as he later told the king. 'O king . . . My God sent his angel, and he shut the mouths of the lions' (vv. 21-22). But he had to be willing to face the lions first! And that couldn't have been easy.

As believers we all have, from to time, our lions' den; some situation or circumstance from which we long to be delivered. Such an experience is part of the cost of discipleship. The Lord Jesus never promised us an armchair existence, but told us to count the cost involved in following him. There is a price to pay, sometimes in full, when God chooses for whatever reason known to him not to deliver us, and sometimes in part, as happened with Daniel when God did deliver him.

There are two things to keep in mind. First, are we willing to pay the price? Are we willing for our Christian discipleship to cost us something in terms of personal sacrifice or pain or loss or in any other way? How great the price we pay must be left with God, but he wants us to show our willingness. Second, when the lions' den has to be faced and God chooses not to deliver us *from* it, then he will deliver us *in* it. That is to say, he will give us grace and strength to gain the victory in our own heart, so that we defeat the circumstance rather than the circumstance defeating us. We are told in verse 23, 'Daniel was lifted from the den . . . because he had trusted in his God'. And God likewise will 'lift' us up in our soul and spirit high above every trial and situation if we put our trust wholly in him.

# 25
# Belshazzar
## who went too far

*Read Daniel 5*

Whenever we hear the expression 'the writing is on the wall', we understand it to mean that some unpleasant consequence is to follow, such as losing one's job or the break-up of a marriage. That is because the expression comes from the story of Belshazzar, who did in fact experience a supernatural writing on the wall of his palace, and shortly afterwards lost his life and his kingdom.

## Human contrasts

Belshazzar was the son, or possibly the grandson, of the great king Nebuchadnezzar whose story is told in the earlier chapters of Daniel. The difference between the two kings is one of stark contrast. Nebuchadnezzar resisted the moving of God's Spirit at several points in his life, but eventually he repented of his pride and came to a good end with the blessing of God upon him.

> Now I, Nebuchadnezzar, praise and exalt and glorify the King of heaven, because everything he does is right and all his ways are just. And those who walk in pride he is able to humble (Daniel 4:37).

Belshazzar, on the other hand, resisted God throughout his life and ended his days under the destructive power of God's judgment.

In his commentary on Daniel, Ronald S. Wallace makes the interesting point that we have several of these contrasting figures in the history of the Bible.

> Along with Abel, for example, we have Cain who hated God and committed murder. Along with Jacob, who after his long struggles ultimately surrendered to God, we have Esau. Along with David there is Saul. Alongside the eleven faithful disciples there is Judas.

And we might add, along with Zacchaeus the rich tax-collector who accepted salvation in Christ, we have the rich young ruler who rejected it because his wealth meant so much to him.

The Lord Jesus summed up these contrasting attitudes within the divine-human relationship with a picture of two ways. There is a broad way along which the crowds heedlessly travel, but it leads ultimately to destruction; and there is the narrow way followed only by the few, but which leads to eternal life (Matthew 7:13-14).

The apostle Paul says the same thing in a different way in his letter to the Colossians:

> See to it that no-one takes you captive through hollow and deceptive philosophy, which depends on human tradition and the basic principles of this world rather than on Christ (Colossians 2:8).

He is contrasting two interpretations of life. There is the human approach, which he calls a 'hollow and deceptive philosophy', because it is man-centred, it is empty and superficial and has no place for God. Today we call it secular humanism. And then there is the revelation of God's truth in Christ and his gospel. These are the only two options open to us; we choose one or the other.

## Contempt for God

The story of Belshazzar opens with a drunken orgy:

> Belshazzar gave a great banquet for a thousand of his nobles and drank wine with them. While Belshazzar was drinking his wine, he gave orders to bring in the gold and silver goblets that Nebuchadnezzar his father had taken from the temple in Jerusalem, so that the king and his nobles, his wives and his concubines might drink from them . . . As they drank the wine, they praised the gods of gold and silver, of bronze, iron, wood and stone (Daniel 5:1-4).

Here is the spectacle of a man showing a deliberate, unrestrained contempt for God and the things of God. As the evening wears on, and the guests at the king's banquet lose their inhibitions under the influence of drink and their behaviour deteriorates, Belshazzar has the brilliant idea of bringing in the sacred vessels taken by Nebuchadnezzar from the temple at Jerusalem and using them as drinking cups. As they drank, they sang their lewd songs to their own Babylonian idols. It was, on Belshazzar's part, a deliberate act of profanity intended to show his subjects his utter contempt for God.

That is always the mark of an individual or a society in danger of reaching the point of no return so far as the patience and forgiveness of God are concerned. It is no longer a matter of ignoring God's claim upon us in the Lord Jesus Christ, but the hostility goes a step further and deliberately despises God and treats him as if he were of no account. This is a feature of our deteriorating society today. TV programmes are littered with nauseating profanities and gutter language of the worst kind, which do not add in any way to the meaningful content of the story but are deliberately inserted as an offence towards God and the people of God. Programme-makers go out of their way to ridicule everything that is sacred and godly.

We must be careful, however, to make it clear that a person loses out on God's salvation and comes under his judgment not because of blasphemous and profane behaviour like that of Belshazzar. It was not his drunkenness or godlessness or even his blasphemy that caused him to perish, since God in mercy and grace can save a man from all those sins. What brought about his damnation was his deliberate rejection of God in his life, and that is always the ultimate blasphemy. Moreover, that is something anyone can be guilty of. People may live a perfectly respectable life in every way and never be heard to utter a blasphemous remark or commit a profane act. But as long as God has no place in their thinking they are as guilty as Belshazzar was. Their whole attitude is an arrogant assertion that they have no need of God and can live independently of his goodness and power, his love and care. They are saying in effect; 'I control my own destiny and believe in my own powers of body and mind. I recognize no other power outside of myself.' That is the ultimate blasphemy, to treat God as of no account and to reject his rightful claim upon us as our Creator and Saviour in the Lord Jesus Christ.

### God's intervention

The drunken Belshazzar and his guests quickly sobered up when God himself suddenly intervened by sending him a message miraculously written on the wall of his palace.

Suddenly the fingers of a human hand appeared and wrote on the plaster of the wall, near the lampstand in the royal palace. The king watched the hand as it wrote. His face turned pale and he was so frightened that his knees knocked together and his legs gave way (vv.5-6).

This is a picture of a man gripped with terror in the depths of his soul, who is beginning to realise that God is not to be trifled with. As the apostle Paul says: 'Do not be deceived: God cannot be mocked. A man reaps what he sows' (Galatians 6:7). The situation is dramatically changed. Gone is Belshazzar's arrogant attitude, and in the place of the raucous noise and lewd songs to the idols of Babylon there is a petrified silence amongst the guests at the banquet. Belshazzar senses that he has gone a step too far in his contempt for God, and that judgment is imminent.

Can we take a step too far where God's patience is concerned, so that the door of salvation is closed to us? The answer of the Bible is yes, we can! In Genesis we are told: 'Then the LORD said, "My Spirit will not contend with man for ever"' (Genesis 6:3). Later in verse 7 God says: 'I will wipe mankind, whom I have created, from the face of the earth . . .' It is clear that human depravity at that stage in the world's history had increased to such an extent that God withdrew his Spirit, not because he was unwilling to save mankind but because man resisted the Spirit's witness and refused to be saved. In Romans chapter 1 we have a similar picture. Three times in verses 24, 26 and 28 Paul uses the expression 'God gave them over', meaning that because of man's depravity and resistance to his truth God lost patience and took off the restraints on sin, saying in effect: 'If you think you can run your life and your world without me, then get on with it and see the mess you will make of things.' The truth is we dare not presume on the unlimited patience and mercy of God where sin and rebellion are concerned. James Philip in his Bible notes quotes the following lines:

> There is a time, we know not when,
> A place we know not where,
> That marks the destiny of man
> In glory or despair.
>
> There is a line, by us unseen,
> That crosses every path,
> The hidden boundary between
> God's patience and His wrath.

Belshazzar crossed that line. What made his resistance so intolerable was the fact that he had been given an opportunity earlier in his life to come to the knowledge of God. When Daniel was eventually brought in to interpret the writing on the wall for the king, he reminds him of how God had moved in the life of his father, king Nebuchadnezzar.

> O king, the Most High God gave your father Nebuchadnezzar sovereignty and greatness and glory and splendour . . . But when his heart became arrogant and hardened with pride, he was deposed from his royal throne and stripped of his glory . . . until he acknowledged that the Most High God is sovereign over the kingdoms of men . . . But you his son, O Belshazzar, have not humbled yourself, though you knew all this. Instead, you have set yourself up against the Lord of heaven (vv.18-23).

Notice Daniel's words, 'you knew all this'. Belshazzar was without excuse. He had been brought up as a child in the Babylonian court and had witnessed God's power in the episode of the lions' den, and the three young men in the fiery furnace, and the merciful dealing of God with his father Nebuchadnezzar when he repented of his sin. Yet in spite of all that he continued to resist God in his life. The writing on the wall, therefore, was the end of what had been a long process of rebellion towards God.

There are many people who are likewise without excuse and are in danger of crossing that line between 'God's patience and His wrath'. It is not as though people in our country have not had the opportunity to hear the gospel of God's salvation in the Lord Jesus Christ. The Bible is an open book; it is readily available, and folk are free to attend God's house whenever they choose to do so. If men continue to trifle with God, therefore, and to resist his grace in salvation, they are running the grave risk that they may exhaust God's patience with them and the opportunity for salvation may pass.

## A word of judgment

Under the leading of God's Spirit Daniel interpreted for the king the divine inscription on the wall.

MENE, MENE, TEKEL, PARSIN.
This is what these words mean:
*Mene:* God has numbered the days of your reign and brought it to an end.
*Tekel:* You have been weighed on the scales and found wanting.
*Peres:* Your kingdom is divided and given to the Medes and Persians.

(vv. 25-28)

We then read in the last verse that, on the very night that word of divine judgment was spoken, the army of Darius the Mede swept in and put an end both to the life and the kingdom of Belshazzar, and he went out of this world a lost soul to meet with God. The writing on the wall contains a word of warning to us too.

(a) 'God has numbered the days.' That is true of all of us. Our days are numbered in God's sight. Some put off the thought of their having to meet with God as though life goes on for ever. But it doesn't. Compared with eternity this life is very short, and a day comes for all of us when we shall leave this world and have to meet with God.

(b) 'You have been weighed on the scales and found wanting.' From the time we were born our whole life has been in the scales of God's reckoning. Men may treat the gospel of Jesus with contempt and live and act as though it were irrelevant, but all the time God is weighing them up, and he overlooks and forgets nothing. There is a sense in which we are all 'found wanting', since we are all sinners in need of God's forgiveness and salvation. The difference is, some recognise this and do something about it by turning to God.

(c) 'Your kingdom is divided and given to the Medes and Persians.' Belshazzar not only lost an earthly kingdom, but the heavenly kingdom was closed to him. The door into God's kingdom through the Lord Jesus Christ is still open to people in this life, however contemptuous they may have been of spiritual things in the past. This is still the day of God's grace, and salvation is there for those who, in repentance and in faith, reach out and accept it.

# 26
# Elihu
## a young man speaks

*Read Job 32:1–33:7*

The main body of the book of Job is taken up with the dialogues between Job and his three friends, Eliphaz, Bildad and Zophar. They attempt to comfort Job in his sufferings but are not very successful because of their judgmental attitude. We are all familiar with the expression 'a Job's comforter', meaning a cold, heartless kind of comforter. But in chapter 32 a fourth friend, Elihu, appears on the scene; he is altogether different from the other three and seems to get closer to Job in his sufferings. He's a bit brash and outspoken, and has a lot to say, since he doesn't stop talking for the next six chapters, but for all that he seems a very attractive personality and we can't help liking him.

## A young man

One big difference between Elihu and the other friends of Job is the fact that he is younger than they are. How young we can't say, but he himself seems to suggest a considerable age difference.

> So Elihu son of Barakel the Buzite said: 'I am young in years, and you are old; that is why I was fearful, not daring to tell you what I know. I thought, "Age should speak;

advanced years should teach wisdom." But it is the spirit
in a man, the breath of the Almighty, that gives him
understanding. It is not only the old who are wise, not
only the aged who understand what is right' (Job 32:6-9).

He is quite right when he says that it is not only older people
who are wise and have understanding and know what is
right. I suppose that is how it should be since, as we grow
older, we should profit from our experience and have a deeper
understanding of life. But it is not always like that, and there
is more than a grain of truth in the saying, 'no fool like an old
fool'. A man with the passing of the years may attain greatness in other directions and reach the top in his field, being
highly qualified to wrestle with the most difficult technical
problems; and yet he may be woefully ignorant in spiritual
understanding of the things of God and of the underlying
purpose and meaning of life itself.

That is why Elihu says that being young is no reason why
he should remain silent any longer when Job and his three
friends have been discussing Job's affliction. He too has a
contribution to make which arises out of his own relationship with God. 'I thought, "Age should speak; advanced
years should teach wisdom." But it is the spirit in a man, the
breath of the Almighty, that gives him understanding' (Job
32:7-8). There is a wisdom or understanding that is indepen-
dent of age and experience and human knowledge; it is the
result of the indwelling Spirit of God within us, giving us
insight and understanding of God's ways and purposes in
the world. In chapter 28 Job says: 'The fear of the Lord—that
is wisdom, and to shun evil is understanding' (v.28). In the
New Testament this is called having 'the mind of Christ'
(1 Corinthians 2:16), which is an insight into life that is open
to both young and old alike.

In his first letter to Timothy Paul says to him:

> Command and teach these things. Don't let anyone look down on you because you are young, but set an example for the believers in speech, in life, in love, in faith and in purity (1 Timothy 4:11-12).

It seems that Timothy was in the habit of allowing some in the church to undermine his authority as the pastor, but Paul reminds him that his authority and spiritual understanding are not related to his age but to the depth and reality of his faith in the Lord Jesus Christ. That should be an encouragement to all young Christians, whether young in years or young in their faith. God wants the contribution that young people can make to the work of the gospel. He wants their youth, their vitality, their energy and enthusiasm.

## An angry young man

It is evident that Elihu was a very angry young man.

> But Elihu . . . became very angry with Job for justifying himself rather than God. He was also angry with the three friends, because they had found no way to refute Job . . . But when he saw that the three men had nothing more to say, his anger was aroused (Job 32:2-5).

He is like a boiling pot and appears to be angry with everyone and everything around him. It all arises, of course, out of his zeal and burning enthusiasm for the things of God. He feels that God's honour is at stake because of some of the things Job has said, and because the three friends have not succeeded in defending God's character. But we get the impression that, if Elihu is not careful, his feelings will get the better of him, and if that happens he will not be of much use as God's spokesman or of much help to Job. And that can sometimes be the danger for young people in the Christian life; their feelings of zeal and enthusiasm can run away with them and make them very angry with everyone and every-thing around them. They get angry with older Christians, who appear rigid and inflexible and 'stick-in-the-mud', and angry with their local church when it seems slow to respond to change, such as making worship more exciting and stimu-lating.

But young people have to remember that older folk are sometimes sceptical of their zeal and enthusiasm because, being young, they have not yet proved that their zeal for the things of God is genuine and lasting and will not blow itself out in the short term. Let's go back for the moment to Paul's advice to Timothy. 'Don't let anyone look down on you because you are young . . .' But how is Timothy to prevent that happening? How is he to get older folk in the church to take him seriously and listen to what he has to say and accept the contribution he has to make to the work of God? Paul's answer is: 'set an example for the believers in speech, in life, in love, in faith and in purity'. Young believers must prove to older Christians, by their conduct and godliness of character and depth of faith, that they can be taken serious-ly, that their enthusiasm and zeal is not of the 'fizzy' variety which quickly blows itself out, and that they have a real contribution to make in the work of the gospel of Jesus Christ.

## An inner compulsion

Whatever his faults, one very attractive feature of Elihu's character is his overwhelming sense of the presence of God within him. Speaking of the three friends he says this:

They are dismayed and have no more to say; words have failed them. Must I wait, now that they are silent? . . . I too will have my say; I too will tell what I know. For I am full of words, and the spirit within me compels me; inside I am like bottled-up wine, like new wineskins ready to burst. I must speak and find relief; I must open my lips and reply. I will show partiality to no-one, nor will I flatter any man; for if I were skilled in flattery, my Maker would soon take me away (vv.15-22).

This is a graphic picture of a young man under a great inner compulsion by the Spirit of God to speak as the Spirit leads. It isn't just a personal opinion he has to give, but a word inspired by the Almighty. He says he will not speak words to 'flatter any man', or God his Maker would be displeased with him. So great is this inner constraint to be a spokesman for God that he says he is like a bottle of new wine about to burst.

It reminds us of two other men under a similar compulsion to declare God's Word. At one point in his prophetic ministry Jeremiah was tempted to give up speaking to the people on God's behalf. But it was no use—he couldn't keep quiet: 'But if I say, "I will not mention him or speak any more in his name," his word is in my heart like a fire . . . shut up in my bones. I am weary of holding it in; indeed, I cannot' (Jeremiah 20:9). And Paul says: 'Yet when I preach the gospel, I cannot boast, for I am compelled to preach. Woe to me if I do not preach the gospel!' (1 Corinthians 9:16).

There is a sense in which that is true of all Christians. We ought to feel an inner compulsion to speak to others of what God in Christ has done in our lives. If an opportunity arises to speak and witness we should feel the Holy Spirit within us urging us to seize the moment before it passes; not in any pressurised manner but quietly and courteously, relying entirely upon God's leading.

## God's spokesman

As we move into chapter 33 we find Elihu still thinking of himself as God's spokesman. 'But now, Job, listen to my words; pay attention to everything I say. I am about to open my mouth; my words are on the tip of my tongue' (vv.1-2). He then touches on three things that should characterise anyone who speaks to others of God, whether they be a preacher in a pulpit or the ordinary Christian in everyday witness.

(a) First, there must be sincerity. Elihu says to Job: 'My words come from an upright heart . . .' (v.3). He means simply that he believes fervently in what he is about to say. If a preacher doesn't genuinely believe in the gospel message he is bringing to others, people instinctively sense his lack of sincerity. One of the most pitiable things in the Church today is the number of ministers who have long since lost their conviction of the authority of the Word of God they are called upon to preach. We must believe in our message, and preach it with such fervency that people are in no doubt that to us it is a great reality and the very revelation of God in the Lord Jesus Christ. Peter says, 'If anyone speaks, he should do it as one speaking the very words of God' (1 Peter 4:11).

(b) Second, people must not only know that we believe the truth we are speaking to them about, but also that we have experienced that truth in our own lives. Elihu says: '. . . my lips sincerely speak what I know' (v.3). He is saying here, in a different way, what he said earlier about wisdom and understanding being the result of the Spirit of God within us. If the people to whom we are witnessing are not aware that the salvation in Christ of which we speak is something we know personally, then it is not likely to have much effect upon them. 'My lips sincerely speak what I know' reminds us of the lines in Wesley's hymn:

> What we have felt and seen
> With confidence we tell.

The confidence rests not in our own powers of persuasion in speaking, but in the inward assurance of sins forgiven and the hope of eternal life.

(c) Third, speaking with confidence is one thing, but we must never give those to whom we witness the impression that we are somehow different from them because God has saved us, and that we are now experts in the matter of salvation. Elihu, for all his hot-headedness, shows a very humble spirit when he says to Job, 'I am just like you before God; I too have been taken from clay . . . nor should my hand be heavy upon you' (vv.6-7). Like Job he too shares in the frailty of human nature—clay—and has no intention of being 'heavy-handed' or censorious, or of adopting a 'holier-than-thou' attitude.

We must make it perfectly clear when we speak to people that we too are sinners who share in the same human weaknesses, but that we are sinners saved by God's grace. What God has done in us he can do in them. They can have the same forgiveness of sins, the same anointing of the Holy Spirit, the same certainty of a home in heaven, if only they will turn to God in repentance and faith in the saving work of the Lord Jesus Christ.